T0328707

Cambridge Elements ≡

Elements in The Global Middle Ages
edited by
Geraldine Heng
University of Texas at Austin
Susan J. Noakes
University of Minnesota – Twin Cities

THE CHERTSEY TILES, THE CRUSADES, AND GLOBAL TEXTILE MOTIFS

Amanda Luyster
College of the Holy Cross

CAMBRIDGE
UNIVERSITY PRESS

Shaftesbury Road, Cambridge CB2 8EA, United Kingdom

One Liberty Plaza, 20th Floor, New York, NY 10006, USA

477 Williamstown Road, Port Melbourne, VIC 3207, Australia

314–321, 3rd Floor, Plot 3, Splendor Forum, Jasola District Centre,
New Delhi – 110025, India

103 Penang Road, #05–06/07, Visioncrest Commercial, Singapore 238467

Cambridge University Press is part of Cambridge University Press & Assessment,
a department of the University of Cambridge.

We share the University's mission to contribute to society through the pursuit of
education, learning and research at the highest international levels of excellence.

www.cambridge.org
Information on this title: www.cambridge.org/9781009485982

DOI: 10.1017/9781009353168

First published 2023

A catalogue record for this publication is available from the British Library

ISBN 978-1-009-48598-2 Hardback
ISBN 978-1-009-35317-5 Paperback
ISSN 2632-3427 (online)
ISSN 2632-3419 (print)

Cambridge University Press & Assessment has no responsibility for the persistence
or accuracy of URLs for external or third-party internet websites referred to in this
publication and does not guarantee that any content on such websites is, or will
remain, accurate or appropriate.

The Chertsey Tiles, the Crusades, and Global Textile Motifs

Elements in The Global Middle Ages

DOI: 10.1017/9781009353168
First published online: December 2023

Amanda Luyster
College of the Holy Cross
Author for correspondence: Amanda Luyster, aluyster@holycross.edu

Abstract: While visual cultures mingled comfortably along the silk roads and on the shores of the Mediterranean, medieval England has sometimes been viewed – by both medieval and more recent writers – as isolated. In this Element, the author introduces new evidence to show that this understanding of medieval England's visual relationship to the rest of the world demands revision. An international team led by the author has completed a digital reconstruction of the so-called Chertsey combat tiles (sophisticated pictorial floor tiles made c. 1250, England), including both images and lost Latin texts. Grounded in the discoveries made while completing this reconstruction, the author proposes new conclusions regarding the historical circumstances within which the Chertsey tiles were commissioned and their significant connections with global textile traditions.

Keywords: medieval, global, art history, England, decorative arts

ISBNs: 9781009485982 (HB), 9781009353175 (PB), 9781009353168 (OC)
ISSNs: 2632-3427 (online), 2632-3419 (print)

Contents

Introduction

Along trade routes, in cities, and in courtly environments, the medieval world was surprisingly cosmopolitan. While visual cultures mingled comfortably along the silk roads and on the shores of the Mediterranean, medieval England has sometimes been viewed – by both medieval and more recent writers – as isolated.[1] When art historians have seen connections between medieval England and other cultures, such connections were generally to nearby kingdoms, predominantly France. Indeed, historical and art historical links between England and France (and other European countries) are well supported. In this Element, I introduce new evidence to show that when we look beyond the canonical fields of architecture and manuscripts, the current under-standing of England's visual relationship to the rest of the world is at best incomplete. I argue that in shifting the focus away from well-known artifacts like architecture and manuscripts to less prestigious objects such as floor tiles and textiles, a new network of connections becomes visible between medieval England and the world beyond Western Europe. As I show, the so-called Chertsey combat tiles, molded ceramic tiles of rare high quality depicting secular subjects made around 1250 and found at Chertsey Abbey in Surrey, were informed by both historical and material engagement with Islamic and Byzantine worlds.[2] Aspects of the Chertsey tiles' visual program connect to iconographic motifs – including royal lion hunts and the Parthian shot, which recur along the silk roads and reappear as far away as medieval Japan – that visually define the English as militarily successful and divinely approved rulers and heirs to the traditions of empire.[3]

Some of the Chertsey tiles' iconographic motifs, like lion hunts and mounted kings and soldiers within roundels, also occur on luxury silks made in the eastern Mediterranean by Islamic and Byzantine craftspeople. Imported silks may have been foundational in inspiring the visual language of the Chertsey combat tiles, and such silks regularly appeared alongside and offered comple-mentary visual language in the same spaces in which the tiles were appreciated. Another Element has laid out the global investments of textiles in the Middle Ages and the prestige and high financial value of luxury medieval silks.[4] Islamic and Byzantine silks were among the most significant carriers of combat icon-ography in medallions, and imported silks bearing the same motifs as the

---

[1] English writers from the sixth century to the thirteenth spoke of themselves as living at the edge of the world: Mittman, *Maps and Monsters in Medieval England*, 16–23. A sense of isolation is reflected in the scholarly term for this field of medieval art history: "Insular art."

[2] See Section 1 for references for the Chertsey tiles.

[3] Hu, "Global Medieval at the 'End of the Silk Road'," 182–183.

[4] Blessing, Shea, and Williams, *Medieval Textiles across Eurasia*.

Chertsey combat tiles – armed knights on horseback and men fighting lions – are witnessed in thirteenth-century English royal and ecclesiastical collections.[5] Imported textiles were regularly hung on walls and covered furnishings in English interiors, and they were also tailored for use in English dress.

While architecture, architectural decoration, and furnishings are often considered separately in scholarship, for medieval visitors, these different elements of a well-appointed interior were perceived as part of an ensemble. When accompanied by silks bearing comparable iconography in an interior space, the tiles would have operated as parts of an experiential whole, as different visual expressions but assembled from the same components: men and horses and lions in combat, set within roundels arranged in a grid ("medallion") pattern, interspersed with foliate patterns.

Realizing that the history and material productions of Islamic and Byzantine worlds are foundational in at least some expressions of medieval English authority has both historical and contemporary implications. First, the gradual expansion of England into a global empire is fully consistent with these early evocations of global destiny and reach. This Element then provides a prologue to the long tale of the English empire and colonialism that plays out across later centuries. Second, and perhaps more importantly, this Element serves to counter long-lived popular mythologies about English isolationism that drive contemporary political impulses. White nationalism has incorporated ideas of Arthur and the English Middle Ages within the problematic fantasy of an island nation which is, always has been, and always should remain independent.[6] My work, grounded in an earlier historical moment, provides a necessary counter-narrative that shows the English have relied for many centuries upon ideas and materials from outside their borders in order to define their sense of authority, history, and future.

The Chertsey combat series tiles are among the most admired medieval floor tiles made anywhere.[7] Yet they were unearthed as a pile of fragments, with no tiles in situ, and most broken into multiple pieces. They were found at Chertsey Abbey intermingled with fragments from two additional Chertsey tile series: the Tristan series, a group of roundels comparable in size to the combat roundels but depicting the Arthurian knight Tristan and surrounded by Anglo-Norman text, and the zodiac series, smaller roundels showing the signs of the zodiac and labors of the months, unaccompanied by text. While heretofore the British Museum had physically reconstructed two roundels from the Chertsey combat

---

[5] See Section 5 and, for more details, the forthcoming book Luyster, *English Bodies, Imported Silks*.

[6] Kim, "White Supremacists"; Albin et al., *Whose Middle Ages*; Ellard, *Anglo-Saxon(ist) Pasts, PostSaxon Futures*.

[7] See chapter 1 for references.

series tiles showing King Richard I the Lionheart (1157–1199) dispatching Saladin (1137– 1193), the sultan of Egypt and Syria (Figure 1), the remainder exist primarily as hundreds of fragments in museum storage drawers (Figure 2).[8] In 1980, British Museum tile curator Elizabeth Eames published hand-drawn black-and-white reconstructions of the images in each roundel and drawings of the fragments of Latin text.[9] However, the incredibly fragmentary nature of the Chertsey tiles has meant that their full impact has not been understood.

An international team which I led has recently completed a digital reconstruction of the entire combat tile program, including both images and lost Latin texts (Figure 3).[10] Our reconstruction reveals that the Chertsey combat tiles do

Figure 1 Roundels depicting Richard the Lionheart and Saladin, combat series tiles found at Chertsey Abbey, molds designed in the 1250s. British Museum 1885,1113.9051–9060 and 1885,1113.9065–9070. © The Trustees of the British Museum

---

[8] Loomis, "Richard Coeur de Lion"; Whatley, "Romance, Crusade," 190–191.

[9] Eames, *Catalogue*.

[10] Essential to our team were faculty, staff, and students at the College of the Holy Cross: notably Janis Desmarais, Martina Umunna '18, Neel Smith, and Therese Starshak '17. I am also most grateful to Beverley Nenk, ceramics curator at the British Museums, as well as Lloyd de Beer and Naomi Speakman, also medieval curators at the British Museum, for aiding me in accessing and thinking about the tiles in the British Museum collection. Emma Warren at the Chertsey Museum, Euan Roger at the National Archives (Kew), and individuals at Winchester Cathedral, the Guildford Museum, and the Chertsey Society have all kindly aided our efforts.

Figure 2 Fragments of Chertsey combat series tiles held at the British Museum, molds designed in the 1250s. Photos: Amanda Luyster

not simply portray what Eames called "a series of famous combats."[11] Instead they present a literary and learned compilation of Crusaders and lion hunters, including biblical heroes, fighting in the Holy Land alongside King Richard the Lionheart. This series of tile images and texts seems to have been an original composition, emphasizing Richard's victory in the Crusades and employing allusions to other kinds of heroic actions, ranging from lion hunts to juridical trials, many of which take on specific meaning in the context of the Crusades.[12] Because art depicting the Crusades made during the period when Crusades to the Holy Land were actively being pursued, c. 1100–1300, is surprisingly rare, this suggests that the Chertsey tiles are even more significant than scholars have previously recognized. While the tiles depict King Richard the Lionheart and his deeds in the 1190s, they bore contemporary import for the Crusading aims of the English king Henry III about sixty years later, around 1250. King Henry III was Richard's nephew, and Henry has previously been considered the patron of the Chertsey combat tiles. I explore the possibility that they were commissioned instead by Henry's queen, Eleanor of Provence, for the first so-called Antioch chamber in her rooms at Westminster Palace. In this royal setting, the combat

---

[11] Eames, *Catalogue*, 1: 144–146.   [12] Luyster, *Bringing the Holy Land Home.*

Figure 3 Photographic composite showing roundels surrounded by partial texts. Digital reconstruction of the Chertsey combat tile mosaic pavement as it could have looked when laid in the thirteenth century. © Janis Desmarais and Amanda Luyster

tiles would have served as positive publicity constructing Henry III as the typological heir of his uncle, the Crusading king Richard. Such an heir was desperately needed after the capture of the French king, Louis IX, in the spring of 1250, during the Seventh Crusade. Louis' capture created a mid-thirteenth-century historical narrative in need of a new Crusader hero.

Our new reconstruction of the combat tile program also enables us to see the Chertsey floor tiles as witnesses to a thirteenth-century English fascination with Islamic and Byzantine textiles. Both the floor's "medallion" design and its iconographic motifs resemble luxury silks imported from Byzantium and Islamic lands (Figures 40–45). The production and weaving of silk, originating in Asia, had become part of Roman, Byzantine, and Sasanian cultures and was later adopted by nascent Islamic realms. Medallion-patterned silks made in Byzantine and Islamic workshops traveled and inspired local works in many places around the globe, especially along the silk roads, a phenomenon which previous scholars have explored.[13] Medallion silks bearing images of combats and roundels – expensive, technically demanding to weave, and portable – were also among the most prized souvenirs brought home by Crusaders returning from their time spent in West Asia and North Africa. I have identified examples of these textiles in English thirteenth-century inventories, affirming that they were present as artistic models in the time and place in which the Chertsey tile pavement was made.[14]

Until now, English interests in and imitations of medallion-style silks have remained largely unrecognized in scholarship. This is partly due to medieval art history's conventional focus on English architecture and English manuscripts, which show less substantial stylistic connections between England and the eastern Mediterranean than other media in the thirteenth century. And yet the Chertsey tiles convey an image of English political and religious superiority in the eastern Mediterranean through a visual composition (medallion pattern) carried by a medium (silk) originally created far outside England. Military and spiritual convictions did not, apparently, stand in the way of English recognition of the visual power and appeal of the cultural heritage of the lands they so fervently desired to control.

My approach is informed by the idea of the "glocal," a word coined to reflect the insistent and even structuring presence of the global within local contexts.[15] Rather than seeing global and local as antithetical, the term glocal recognizes that these

---

[13] Canepa, "Textiles and Elite Tastes"; Gasparini, "Sino-Iranian Textile Patterns"; Blessing, "Draping, Wrapping, Hanging"; Anderlini, "Dressing the Sacred"; Gasparini, *Transcending Patterns*; Blessing et al., *Medieval Textiles across Eurasia*.

[14] See Section 5. In addition, I am currently completing a book project, tentatively entitled *English Bodies, Imported Silks: The Impact of Islamic and Byzantine Textiles in Gothic England*, with further details.

[15] The sociologist Roland Robertson brought the term "glocalization," a portmanteau of globalization and local, to the attention of the English-speaking world in the 1990s. Glocalization attends to the presence of the global within the local. See Robertson, "Glocalization: Time-Space and Homogeneity-Heterogeneity"; Robertson, "Glocalization."

spheres depend upon and indeed partly construct each other. The medallion-style images of kings, lions, and combats on the Chertsey tiles are informed by the transregional distribution of silks; the widely distributed silks are actually only used and understood in local environments, including abbeys and palaces along the Thames. The global always only appears in local circumstances.

Planting our feet on English soil and then taking a global perspective, one that extends beyond France or Western Europe, enables us to see previously unrecognized connections to and distinctions from foreign artifacts, like medallion textiles. The connection is that medieval English men and women were also fascinated by collecting, gifting, and imitating medallion textiles with images of combats. The distinction is that the patron of the Chertsey tiles chose to commission a work in local ceramic rather than imported silk, in a design which adopts but also subtly distorts patterns found on medallion silks. The rationale behind this decision is examined in the conclusion: I suggest that silks held both positive (luxurious and imperial) and negative (foreign and feminizing) associations in England. Therefore, manufacturing a silk-derived design in practical ceramic could thus reference the luxurious and imperial connotations of silks while avoiding suggestions of hubris or excess.

The designer of the tiles made a single combat motif the focus of each roundel, while in some woven designs the combat motifs are doubled across axes of symmetry within each roundel. The Chertsey tiles also show a separation into individual roundels of motifs that are often conjoined in a single roundel in medallion textiles: kings on horseback, the Parthian shot, the lion hunt, and war. The separate roundels of the Chertsey combat series were nonetheless designed to be understood as a single program. Finally, the clothing and appearance of the protagonists represented on the Chertsey roundels suggest their Western European (probably understood as English) identity. Their clothing, armor, hair, and other markers of cultural identity differ from those represented on imported textiles, whose protagonists would have read as more or less "foreign." These decisions made by the Chertsey tiles' patron and designer make sense when understood in the light of local concerns: available technologies and capabilities surrounding ceramic tile production, ideas about the suitability of silk, and the political utility of proposing the English king as a successful leader of the Crusades in the 1250s.

Much of art history is constructed around a canon of objects which has remained, significantly if not entirely, unchanged over multiple decades. If we want to tell a new story, one in which medieval English and European cultural creations are heavily impacted by events, stories, and objects from outside their own geographical boundaries, we need to anchor ourselves within a different collection of objects. The Chertsey tiles provide a rich and flexible example for generating new global art historical narratives.

1 The Reconstructed Program: Battles in the Holy Land

State of Research

From at least the nineteenth century, the Chertsey tiles, with their 10-inch roundels showing lions and heroes, have been among the most admired medieval floor tiles in England. They have been called the "high-watermark" of medieval tile manufacture and "one of the finest, if not the finest, inlaid pavements in existence."[16] The eminent scholar of medieval tiles, Christopher Norton, maintains that they are "justly famous; as well as being some of the earliest two-color tiles in Europe, they are also incomparably the finest, both technically and artistically, and they have no known parallel on the Continent."[17] The Chertsey tiles have also appeared in a variety of publications on medieval topics, from literary to archaeological to historical in subject.[18] Some authors have proposed that they are significant not just within the limited realm of ceramics but that they are "among the finest examples of medieval art in Britain."[19] Indeed the tiles were included in the well-known exhibition of English medieval art "Age of Chivalry: Art in Plantagenet England 1200–1400," held in 1987–1988 at the Royal Academy of Arts in London.[20] The roundels depicting the duel of Richard and Saladin (Figures 4 and 5) have drawn attention in recent exhibitions in Germany, the United States – including an exhibition I curated in spring 2023 – and elsewhere due to their fine and appealing drawing style and Crusading themes.[21]

The Chertsey combat tiles have had an impact even on nonmedieval scholarship, educational materials, and popular culture. For instance, the Richard and Saladin tiles open an inquiry into the Crusades in the web-based "Teaching History with 100 Objects," completed in 2015 and supported by the UK's Department for Education, which draws from museum collections across Great Britain and Northern Ireland.[22] And in February 1997, the Britpop band Kula Shaker rather unexpectedly used the Chertsey tile showing Richard the

---

[16] Loomis, *Illustrations*, 15; Wight, *Mediaeval Floor Tiles*, 103.

[17] Norton, "The Luxury Pavement," 20.

[18] Perella, *The Kiss Sacred and Profane*, 27–29; Camille, "Gothic Signs and the Surplus," figure 8; Furrow, *Expectations of Romance*, 173, 232, 237.

[19] Greene, *Medieval Monasteries*, 86.   [20] Alexander and Binski, *Age of Chivalry*.

[21] Luyster, *Bringing the Holy Land Home*. Some of the material in this chapter was also presented, in an abbreviated form, in that exhibition catalogue. The exhibition website, including recorded lectures, conference presentations, and interactives, can be accessed at https://chertseytiles .holycross.edu.

[22] http://teachinghistory100.org/about/. The abbey of Chertsey is also used in a classroom activity created by the National Archives: www.nationalarchives.gov.uk/education/resources/chertsey/.

Figure 4 Digital reconstruction of Richard the Lionheart and proposed reconstruction of surrounding text. Chertsey combat series tile, molds designed in the 1250s. Eames design 466. © Janis Desmarais and Amanda Luyster

Figure 5 Digital reconstruction of Saladin and proposed reconstruction of surrounding text. Chertsey combat series tile, molds designed in the 1250s. Eames design 467. © Janis Desmarais and Amanda Luyster

Lionheart as the cover of their release of "Hush," which peaked at No. 2 in the United Kingdom.[23]

Despite the Chertsey tiles' widespread appeal, we know little about them. The tiles were mold-made, and they seem to have been used at multiple sites, although Chertsey is by far the most significant findspot. Nearly all of the tiles were discovered in a pile of broken pieces at Chertsey Abbey; the medieval tile floor may have been destroyed during the sixteenth or seventeenth century.[24] Tiles from the Chertsey combat series were also discovered under the steps at Winchester Cathedral. In both instances, the tiles seem to have been laid in the second half of the thirteenth century. However, it is generally agreed that the original tile molds were likely to have been a royal commission c. 1250 under the patronage of King Henry III of England or his queen, Eleanor of Provence, for a floor at Westminster Palace.[25] Henry III and Eleanor were known for their patronage of fine floors, from the extraordinary Cosmati pavement at Westminster Abbey to the subtly hued tiled floor of the queen's chamber at Clarendon.[26] The Chertsey tiles' quality, secular theme, and drawing style have been convincingly connected to certain tiles that survive in the Westminster Abbey chapter house, which was completed under the patronage of Henry III.

Despite the popularity of the Chertsey combat tiles, scholarship has presented no new interpretations of their significance since 1980. Study of the tiles has been limited by their damaged condition and by meager documentation. Until the completion of our digital reconstruction, scholars interested in the iconography of the Chertsey tiles had to rely on the black-and-white drawings published in Eames' 1980 catalogue, which are still used in the British Museum's online catalogue as the identifying "head shots" for most of the tile fragments.[27] These drawings represent the summation of many years of work on behalf of Eames and her assistants, who had travelled the country looking for fragments. Each drawing incorporated iconography from all of the fragments of each design known to Eames. Due to the highly fragmented state of the tiles, these drawings provided an essential waypoint in deciphering the pavement. However, like all hand-drawings, they are susceptible to various forms of subtle distortion and human error.[28] And while Eames reconstructed the images in each roundel, she did not attempt to reconstruct the text or link any of the text

---

[23] I am grateful to Jim Peters of the British Museum for bringing this album cover to my attention.

[24] Rob Poulton, pers. comm. Mar. 2023 and Poulton, *Archaeological Investigations.*

[25] Alexander et al., *Age of Chivalry*, 181; Eames, *Catalogue*, 1: 163–164; Morrison and Hedeman, *Imagining the Past*, cat. no. 54, note 12; Lethaby, "Romance Tiles," 78–79; Keen, "Chapter House."

[26] Eames, *A Decorated Tile Pavement*; Carpenter, "King Henry III and the Cosmati Work"; Grant and Mortimer, *Westminster Abbey: The Cosmati Pavements.*

[27] Eames, *A Decorated Tile Pavement.*   [28] Hoffman, "Between East and West."

fragments with a particular roundel. The only section of the pavement which had been physically reconstructed is the two roundels with Richard and Saladin, without the Latin texts which would have originally accompanied these roundels, on display at the British Museum.

Our reconstruction of the combat series presents photographic composites of each design in the combat series as well as the Latin inscriptions and foliate ornament that accompanied them (Figure 3). These composites have been digitally constructed from a series of carefully controlled photographs of the fragments at the British Museum taken in the summer of 2017.[29] Each fragment was photographed, then digitally isolated from its background, and manipulated to precisely overlap other fragments in the composite image. Due to the thickness of each roundel, this kind of reconstruction could never be accomplished in the real world. As each fragment is about an inch thick, and as the fragments rarely came from the same tile and hence there is nearly always overlap between the fragments, stacking actual fragments would result in a haphazard-looking leaning tower of ceramics, and not in a legible design. The digital reconstructions, by contrast, create – for the first time – fully accurate renditions of each roundel design.

We follow Elizabeth Eames in identifying fourteen different roundel designs within the combat series.[30] Five of the roundels show combats with lions, including that of Samson, and seven show other combat themes, including two roundels showing Richard and Saladin's duel. The final two fragments are too small for meaningful analysis. In our reconstruction, we have arranged the roundels in an order that seems logical. Even if, however, the roundels were differently ordered, they would read in the same way: the entire floor is a scene of battle in full action that provides a context for the Crusading deeds of Richard the Lionheart. The floor contains events from the past at different times – biblical history, Greco-Roman history, and the more recent history of the Crusades. The roundels showing lion combats reference Richard's "lion heart." They also allude to lion hunts, which were among the characteristic exploits of crusading knights who visited the eastern Mediterranean, where lions live, and where great deeds were understood to be done, both in the past and in the medieval present. Samson and other figures fighting lions function as personifications of strength, both physical and moral, that bolster our

---

[29] Janis Desmarais, with assistance from Martina Umunna, played an essential role in creating the digital reconstruction of the tiles. See her full documentation at https://docs.google.com/docu ment/d/14XsYsPvc0lLFg3tp7dc1yKKMgjhM_kD2DzX02e0O5nY/edit?usp=sharing. I am most grateful to the British Museum and in particular to curator Beverley Nenk for providing access to the tiles.

[30] Eames, *Catalogue*.

impression of Richard's sheer physical might and that of his crossbowmen with their vicious weapons, who shoot arrows across the floor, wounding their opponents. The combatants in all contests, both the soldiers and the lion hunters, are part of a varied but contiguous and continuous struggle that spills across the countryside; men fight other men and beasts; combatants show their God-given courage and superhuman strength. Richard's successful defeat of Saladin joins with the success of the other soldiers in defeating enemies and lions, and divine involvement in selecting the winner of these battles is suggested by the inclusion of a juridical combat.

The visual program of the combat tiles was probably informed by a substantial tradition of literature about the Crusades in which a variety of heroes, biblical and epic, are introduced in the context of the battles in West Asia and North Africa. Iconographic analysis of the Chertsey tile roundels also reveals connections with broader traditions. For instance, for millennia and across continents, from ancient Egypt to Mesopotamia to China, images of kings fighting lions have provided visual metaphors for royal military might in the field.[31] Additionally, one tile represents the Parthian shot, in which a mounted archer turns completely around in the saddle to shoot an enemy behind. This was a well-known military maneuver during the Crusades, practiced by both the Mamluks and the Mongols, among others; on the Chertsey tile, a European or English soldier has adopted and become proficient at a skill practiced by opposing, foreign forces in the Crusades. Only by examining the Chertsey combat tiles in their global context can we reach a more accurate understanding of their meaning.

Richard the Lionheart and Saladin

The heart of the story presented in the Chertsey combat tiles is showcased in the two roundels showing King Richard I the Lionheart's dispatch of Saladin, who is shown falling limply from his weakened horse (Figure 1).[32] Saladin, or Salah ad-Din, was the sultan of Egypt and Syria and the founder of the Ayyubid dynasty, and he led the Muslim military campaign against the Crusader states in the Levant during the Third Crusade. This scene is fictional – not only did Richard never defeat Saladin in single combat, but Richard and Saladin never even met, although they were opponents in the Third Crusade.[33] That Crusade ended with a truce, and Richard returned to France. This mythical English Crusading victory is propaganda that constructs an advantageous view of Richard the Lionheart, and by extension, his nephew, King Henry III.

---

[31] Allsen, *The Royal Hunt.*

[32] Loomis, "Richard Coeur de Lion"; Whatley, "Romance, Crusade," 190–191.

[33] Loomis, "Richard Coeur de Lion"; Prestwich, "Richard Coeur de Lion"; Whatley, "Romance, Crusade," 190.

Within Richard's own lifetime, he had become a semilegendary figure.[34] By the time that the combat tiles were commissioned, only some fifty years after his death, Richard was a popular hero – the first English king since the Norman Conquest to achieve this status.[35] Even today, in the words of John Gillingham, "no other king of England has retained so strong a hold over the imaginations of ordinary English men and women, both children and adults."[36] Richard was not just a king of England; he was, of course, also a prince of European domains, a ruler of the Angevin empire, and, as is frequently noted, spent little time in England. Yet in legends and history from the Middle Ages until the present day, Richard is most often understood as a king of England who went on Crusade. In the combat tiles, Richard is presented as the English Crusading king, *par excellence*.

As J. O. Prestwich has written, it is impossible to separate the Richard of history from the Richard of legend, not only because history and legend (and romance) were not so different in the middle ages but also because Richard himself liked to boast of his exploits.[37] In his confrontation against Philip Augustus, King of France from 1180 to 1223, Richard "claimed to have unhorsed three of his opponents with a single lance."[38] According to Gerald of Wales, Richard claimed that he could hold Chateau-Gaillard against Philip Augustus even if its walls were made of butter.[39] More colorful tales describe how, when Richard was confronted with a lion who was meant to eat him, and armed only with forty silk handkerchiefs, Richard tore the heart out of the lion and ate it.[40] It was said that Richard could have avoided death from an injury sustained by a crossbow bolt had he only followed his doctors' advice and avoided sex.[41] Other stories suggested that Richard enjoyed boiling the heads of "Saracens" – the term used in England to describe Muslim opponents – and serving them at dinner.[42] (Note that in this Element, I will use the term "Saracen," as the medieval English did, to describe their Muslim foes in the Crusades. The English ideological conception of their Muslim opponents often had very little to do with the historical lived realities of medieval Muslims. The so-called Saracens in English writings vary in character but were often stereo-typically greedy or foolish, and their appearance and deeds owe much more to English imagination than they do to historical reality.[43])

---

[34] Stubbs, *Itinerarium peregrinorum et gesta regis Ricardi.*
[35] Gillingham, "Some Legends of Richard," 52.   [36] Ibid., 51.
[37] Prestwich, "Richard Coeur de Lion," 1.   [38] Ibid., 3.   [39] Ibid.
[40] Ibid., 1; Gillingham, "Some Legends of Richard," 55.
[41] Gillingham, "Some Legends of Richard," 57.   [42] Prestwich, "Richard Coeur de Lion," 3.
[43] Calkin, *Saracens*, 1–3.

King Richard the Lionheart has been recognized in this series of tiles for at least a century, identifiable by the combination of his crown, the three lions of England on his shield, and his exotic-looking opponent, who sports clothing associated with Saracens: a pointed cap, a loose tunic instead of an armor, and a large curved sword. Richard on the Chertsey tiles rides intently and mercilessly, balancing the lance between the ears of his horse. His mount moves at a flying gallop, as indicated by the raised front hooves, and Richard uses the tensed strength of his entire body, propelled by his mount, to thrust the lance into the body of his enemy. The wounded Saladin, discomfited and uncomfortable, slides gracelessly from his mount, the tip of Richard's lance extending behind him, while his horse regards us with two large, staring eyes. As already noted, this event never happened: it is an English fantasy.

The Chertsey design (c. 1250) is the earliest extant image to depict a single combat between Richard and Saladin. A small number of later images also depict this scene, including the Luttrell Psalter (Diocese of Lincoln, c. 1325–1335). It is likely that stories about Richard and Saladin circulated orally, and perhaps the Chertsey duel relies on such a source. Yet despite the constructed and fictional nature of the Chertsey duel, it is a subject that makes sense as a visual summation of a certain (also constructed) Crusade narrative. Richard, the best-known English Crusading king, is pitted against one of the most famous Crusader enemies, Saladin, and wins handily. The pairing alludes to well-known individuals and immediately expresses the military superiority of the English Christian king. Its value as ideological shorthand, whether delivered visually, in text, or in song, seems to render historical accuracy secondary.

Kingship and Bravery: Lion Hunters

The lion fights in roundels adjacent to Richard the Lionheart suggest the sheer strength and military capability of Richard and his associates. Lion hunts were also typical of written and visual narratives about Crusaders. As lions were thought to live in the Holy Land, fighting a lion was a regular event in Crusader chronicles, and combats with lions were also represented on Crusader seals. Lion combats are characteristic not only of Crusading heroes in literature but also of biblical heroes (a fact which is not coincidental: biblical heroes were models for Crusading heroes).

Hunting and lion hunts have long been used as a metaphor for military triumph in the ancient Near East as well as in ancient Greece and Rome.[44] Notably, Assyrian palace reliefs showed thrilling large-scale narratives of kings

---

[44] Feltham, "Lions, Silks and Silver"; Allsen, *The Royal Hunt*; Walker, *The Emperor and the World*, 22, 32–33, and 188, notes 11 and 12.

Figure 6 Wall panel relief depicting King Ashurbanipal hunting a lion. Assyrian, 645–640 BCE. The British Museum. Photo: Istock/Getty Images

fighting lions (Figure 6) in the first millennium BCE, understood to function as visual metaphors for royal military might in battle and to represent the king's power to "tame" wild lands, bringing them under his control.[45] Later civilizations, including the Sasanians (Figure 7), the Byzantines, and the Abbasids, carried on this heritage, and images of lion hunts remain on late antique and Byzantine floor mosaics. The Chertsey lion hunts fit neatly within this tradition: they refer metaphorically to the defeat of enemies as well as to the king's strength and bravery.[46] In the Chertsey program, the presence of lions in the lands where Richard is fighting may also suggest its wild nature, presenting the lands of the eastern Mediterranean as ripe for English conquest and control.

The roundels showing lion combats in the Chertsey combat pavement serve several functions. First, they act within the long history of the use of the lion hunt as a metaphor for military triumph; second, they focus attention on Richard as the mighty "lion heart"; third, they highlight the arms (and possessions) of the royal family of England; fourth, they locate the combats in North Africa and West Asia, with particular relevance in this visual context to the Holy Land and the Crusades.

---

[45] Allsen, *The Royal Hunt*; Brereton, *I am Ashurbanipal*.
[46] Walker, *The Emperor and the World*, 32–33.

Figure 7 Sasanian King Hunting Lions, late 300s CE. Iran, Sasanian, fourth century. Alabaster. The Cleveland Museum of Art, Leonard C. Hanna, Jr. Fund 1963.258

The presence of lions amidst the combats on the floor draws attention to the "lion heart" of Richard the Crusader himself. This moniker had apparently been attributed to Richard during his lifetime: the Norman Ambroise, who traveled with Richard on the Third Crusade and who wrote as an eyewitness, applied the epithet "coeur de lion" to Richard when he first sighted Saladin's camp and Acre in 1191.[47] A thirteenth-century romance explained the origin of the descriptor more colorfully: Richard's adventure with the lion and the forty silk handkerchiefs led to his eating the lion's heart, hence "lionheart," and since then, "lion heart" has been "inseparable from Richard's fame."[48] Tile designs showing men fighting alongside lions visually portray Richard's own superhuman, lion-like strength, also shown in high relief in Richard's apparent defeat of Saladin.

Lions were also associated with royalty and, specifically, with English royalty. Lions had recently come into use as the heraldic identity of English kings, as shown on the shield of Richard on the combat tiles. Richard was the first to bear the arms of three lions, which was then adopted by subsequent English kings, including John and Henry III. Matthew Paris also displays a keen awareness of arms in his Chronicles, in which the death of important individuals is marked by illustrations showing the traditional display of their arms hung

---

[47] Prestwich, "Richard Coeur de Lion," 1.   [48] Ibid.

upside down.[49] Henry also used the lions on his seal and elsewhere.[50] The distribution of the king's seal on important documents throughout the kingdom would have ensured a wide knowledge of the heraldic association between the English royal family and the lion.

Indeed, there was an additional reason for individuals to associate lions with the royal family. Frederick II, the Holy Roman Emperor, had given three lions to Henry in 1235, and they were housed in the Tower of London.[51] It is probably not a coincidence that three lions were given: this number, of course, coincides with the number of lions on the king's arms. Two lions' skulls dated to the medieval period were excavated at the Tower in 1936: these were identified as Barbary lions, which are now extinct in the wild and survive only in zoos.[52] Barbary lions were originally found in North Africa and Egypt, and are closely related to the Asiatic lions found in Palestine and Asia Minor; hence, it is precisely this kind of lion that would have been encountered by Crusaders. Frederick's contacts in these regions due to his role in the Crusades and as King of Jerusalem must have given him access to Barbary lions. Nor were Frederick's lions the first to have been owned by the English royal family. William of Malmesbury, who wrote in the first half of the twelfth century, remarked that lions were among the exotic beasts eagerly sought by King Henry I and kept at his lodge in Woodstock, Oxfordshire.[53] Henry I's menagerie was started in 1125, and beasts descended from this collection may have stocked the menagerie of King John. Henry III inherited John's menagerie, housed at the Tower of London, and it is this "zoo" that would have welcomed and housed the three lions gifted by Frederick. Lions in England, then, were rare, exotic beasts, associated with the lands of the Crusades – and they were owned by the royal family.

The presence of lions among the combats also suggests a location where lions were known to live, perhaps North Africa, Egypt, or Palestine. This coincides with the understood location of the fictional battle between Richard and Saladin, which must have been presumed to take place in the Holy Land, possibly at Arsuf (between Acre and Jaffa), which was the location of a historical battle between the forces led by the two men. Samson's biblical encounter with the lion took place in Palestine, and of course other biblical encounters with lions (as with David or Daniel, for

---

[49] See the inverted arms of Richard I, indicating his death, from a manuscript of the *Chronica Majora* by Matthew Paris, fol. 85v. Thirteenth century. Royal MS 14 C VII.

[50] The Westminster Abbey chapter house pavement, for which Henry III also acted as patron, contained two bands depicting the king's coat of arms (three lions) supported by centaurs, and these bands were "by far the grandest and the most strategically placed," as well as the largest, among the other patterns of tiles. Carpenter, "King Henry III and the Chapter House," 37.

[51] Thomas, "The Tower of London's Royal Menagerie," 30.

[52] Natural History Museum, "Barbary Lion Skull from London," by Lisa Hendry. Consulted March 7, 2021. www.nhm.ac.uk/discover/barbary-lion-skull-from-the-tower-of-london.html.

[53] Thomas, "The Tower of London's Royal Menagerie," 30.

instance) took place in the same region. While the medieval bestiary does not specify where lions can be found, Pliny the Elder (writing in the first-century CE and widespread by medieval times) says that lions lived in select locations in Europe, Syria, and Africa.[54] Indeed, a map of the Holy Land ascribed to Matthew Paris bears a legend in one region, "ubi sunt leones" or "here be lions."[55]

Many Crusaders were said to have met and battled lions while on Crusade.[56] Matthew Paris tells the story of an English Crusader, Hugh de Neville, who accompanied Richard the Lionheart on Crusade in the 1190s and killed a lion in the Holy Land using arrows and a sword (Figure 8).[57] In the previous century, William of Malmesbury wrote of a lion who came upon a soldier on Crusade: the solider managed to defend himself for some time using just his shield.[58] Another early twelfth-century source, the *Historia Iherosolimitana* by Robert the Monk, describes a Crusader who knocked flat and killed a lion with his bare hands.[59]

Figure 8 A lion killed by arrows and a sword. Matthew Paris, *Chronica Majora II*, thirteenth century. Cambridge, Corpus Christi College, MS 016II, fol. 61v. Image courtesy of The Parker Library, Cambridge, Corpus Christi College. Licensed under a Creative Commons Attribution-NonCommercial 4.0 International License

---

[54] Bostock, *Natural History*, book 8, chapter 17.

[55] Pers. comm., April 2023, Nicholas Paul. Oxford, Corpus Christi College, MS 2*.

[56] Hodgson, "Lions, Tigers, and Bears"; Leson, "'Partout la figure du lion'."

[57] Cambridge, Corpus Christi College MS 16, fol. 57v, as cited in Henderson, "Romance and Politics," 31, note 26.

[58] Mynors, Thomson, and Winterbottom, *Gesta regum Anglorum = The History of the English Kings*, 659, iv.373.6.

[59] Sweetenham, *Robert the Monk's History*, 200.

The Chertsey tiles show lion combats that echo these narratives: a lion and a soldier with a shield, a lion and a knight with a sword, and a lion overcome by bare hands. I am not suggesting that the tiles drew directly on these specific scenes in these specific Crusading texts, but rather that there were certain medieval tropes about men fighting lions in particular ways on the Crusades. These tropes would have developed in the space between text, song, and image, and they appear both in extant texts and the Chertsey combat tiles. While viewers today might not associate lion combats with the Crusades, for medieval viewers, lion combats were among a group of events that were said to occur regularly in Crusading narratives. The lion combats, then, are not dissociated from the narrative of Richard and Saladin's battle. These two kinds of fights occur in the same place, albeit not necessarily at the same time.

Lion combats were a visual and textual narrative mechanism for showing the strength and valor of Crusading knights. The same message was conveyed by texts that describe fighting men as "lions." In the *Chanson de Roland*, the Franks are as "fierce as lions."[60] The *Historia Iherosolimitana* compares men to lions in multiple passages: the Duke and his men were like a lion; a man's brothers were next to him like two lions next to a third.[61] The parallel between lions and strength was sufficiently well known for an anonymous English seal matrix (c. 1270–1400) to use the phrase: "I am a strong lion."[62] This inscription was also common on other contemporary seals.[63] The lion combats, due to the locations where lions were known to live, as well as tropes of lion fights on Crusade, connect with other combat scenes to place the location of the floor's action in the eastern Mediterranean and to expand that floor's action from battles against Saracens to battles with other local inhabitants, like lions. Both kinds of battles show the physical might and bravery of Crusaders.

Samson

The figure of Samson is recognizable in Eames 472 (Figure 9) because of his long, tousled hair and characteristic gesture, hands at the lion's mouth, preparing to tear it apart with his bare hands (Judges 14.6). The Chertsey Samson is clean shaven, youthful, with floating locks and a narrow, ornamented band encircling his head. The band may be a reference to Samson's origins and life

---

[60] Knicely, "Food for Thought," 27, note 59, citing the Song of Roland, trans. Glyn Burgess (London, 1990), 89.

[61] Sweetenham, *Robert the Monk's History*, 94; 199.

[62] Seal Matrix SF-E7A3E1 of the Portable Antiquities Scheme, https://finds.org.uk/database/arte facts/record/id/953985. The legend SVM LEO RTIS "stands for the complete version SVM LEO FORTIS," as noted in the online record.

[63] The Portable Antiquities Scheme lists ten other English medieval seal matrices bearing this inscription. See https://finds.org.uk/database/search/results/q/SUM+LEO+FORTIS.

Figure 9 Digital reconstruction of Samson and proposed reconstruction of surrounding text. Chertsey combat series tile, molds designed in the 1250s. Eames design 472. © Janis Desmarais and Amanda Luyster

in the Holy Land: in other images, he is depicted wearing a variety of headgear suggesting his eastern origins.

Medieval readers' and writers' – and artists' and viewers' – understanding of biblical figures, including Samson, was rich and flexible.[64] Samson appears frequently in medieval art alongside other images of men fighting. He also appears as a decorative motif on candlesticks, as a leather stamp on bookbindings, and on game pieces.[65] Significant nodes of meaning for Samson in medieval England include his impressive physical strength, the assimilation of his battle with the lion to the battle between Christ and Satan, and the narrative of his life spent in the Holy Land. His identity as a strong man, a fighter, who lived in the eastern Mediterranean, connects him with the other Chertsey combatants. His presence functions to connect the other Chertsey fighters to biblical history and the Holy Land; he is in some sense their typological forerunner. His well-known combat with a lion links his struggle with that of Richard, the famous lion-heart, whose coat of arms bore lions, as well as with the remaining lion combats.

---

[64] Dinkova-Bruun, "Biblical Thematics."

[65] Mann, "Samson vs. Hercules"; Forsyth, "The Samson Monolith"; Ambrose, "Samson, David, or Hercules."

Man Raising a Club

In the incomplete design known as Eames 463 (Figure 10), an unarmored man in a long tunic raises a weapon above his head, while directing his attention downwards. I suggest that this scene depicts a man raising a club: it could represent either a specific individual who fought a lion with a club, like David, or an anonymous fighter. Many images survive showing David using a club to slay a lion: for instance, a Byzantine plate in the Metropolitan Museum of Art, dating 629–630 (Figure 11), and a manuscript in Evreux dating from 1230. The tenth-century Byzantine Paris Psalter (Figure 12) also contains a richly painted figure of David raising a club against a lion. Next to his club is inscribed the Greek word "Ischys," or "Might," thereby presenting David as a personification of Might. Herakles, the classical strongman, also used a club against the Nemean lion and was sometimes depicted with one. Images of David with a lion and club are more frequently found in medieval Northern Europe than images of Heracles, but either could be reasonably associated with this design. David was also a model biblical king and a prototype for Crusader rulers. Indeed, the Crusader territories were even known as the *Regnum David.*[66]

Figure 10 Digital reconstruction of Chertsey combat tile, man raising a club, and proposed reconstruction of surrounding text. Chertsey combat series tile, molds designed in the 1250s. Eames design 463. © Janis Desmarais and Amanda Luyster

---

[66] Weiss, "Biblical History," 713.

Figure 11 Plate with David slaying a lion. Byzantine, dated 629–630. The Metropolitan Museum of Art, 17.190.394. © The Metropolitan Museum of Art. Image source: Art Resource, NY

Figure 12 David slaying the lion; personification of Might, fol. 2v. The Paris Psalter, Byzantine, tenth century. Paris Bibliotheque Nationale gr. 139. Image: BnF

The larger import of Eames 463 is that it witnesses what is likely to be another lion combat, perhaps that of David, who was a prototype for Crusader kings, and that, yet again – like Samson the Strong – this design can be understood as a representation of great physical strength.

Lion and Standing Knight

A lion rears, scrabbling his claws against a shield held by a standing knight in Eames 470 (Figure 13). The standing knight wears a long tunic over chain mail, his helm is down, and he plants his feet to hold his shield strong against his attacker. He positions his sword low, focusing on defense.

The Eames drawing did not include all extant fragments of this design. London's Victoria & Albert Museum holds another large fragment that we integrated into the composite photograph, thereby adding substantially to the depiction of the lion. This is also one of the few cases in which we note a possible mistake in the Eames drawing: the drawing of Eames 470 shows two chevrons on the knight's shield, whereas our photography shows evidence of only a single chevron.[67]

Figure 13 Digital reconstruction of Chertsey combat tile, lion and standing knight, and proposed reconstruction of surrounding text. Chertsey combat series tile, molds designed in the 1250s. Eames design 470. © Janis Desmarais and Amanda Luyster

---

[67] Janis Desmarais of the College of the Holy Cross noticed the difference in chevrons.

As noted by George Henderson in 1978, this tile design shows a close connection to an English seal whose matrix was probably made in 1235, that of Roger de Quincy, Earl of Winchester and Constable of Scotland 1235–1264.[68] This seal shows a standing knight, sword held low, staunchly supporting his shield against the claws of a rampant lion – just like the combat tile design (Figure 14). The iconography of Roger de Quincy's seal substantially follows that of his father, Saher or Saer, also Earl of Winchester (matrix made c. 1218).[69] I find Henderson's hypothesis that this design derives from a misunderstood copying of either Saher's or Roger's seal reasonable.

However, the imagery of a standing knight fighting a lion was not limited only to seals. In Chretien de Troyes' late-twelfth-century *Roman de Percival*, Gawain fought a lion whose claws stuck in his shield, although this battle took place in a bedroom.[70] The sculpted tympanum of a donjon (c. 1225–1230) belonging to the Coucy family in Picardy also bore the design of a knight on foot fighting a lion (Figure 15).[71] In this case, Richard Leson has connected the iconography of the knight fighting a lion to the presence of lions in the Holy Land and the identity of the Coucy knights as Crusaders.[72]

Figure 14 Seal of Roger de Quincy, Earl of Winchester and Constable of Scotland 1235–1264. After J. H. Stevenson, Heraldry in Scotland. Glasgow: James Maclehose and Sons, 1914. Vol. 1. Plate viii, figure 5

---

[68] I am most grateful to Lloyd de Beer of the British Museum for bringing this connection to my attention. See Henderson, "Romance and Politics"; Alexander et al., *Age of Chivalry*, no. 143.

[69] Henderson, "Romance and Politics," plates 19, 20; Alexander et al., *Age of Chivalry*, no. 143.

[70] Henderson, "Romance and Politics," 31.　　[71] Leson, "'Partout la figure du lion'," 32, note 9.

[72] Ibid., 51–53.

Figure 15 Jacques Androuet du Cerceau, Drawing of the Coucy donjon tympanum, 1576. London, British Museum, Prints and Drawings, Inv. No. U.809. © The Trustees of the British Museum

Saher de Quincy died on Crusade in 1219, probably accompanied by his son, Roger. Henderson also makes the connection between the presence of lions on these seals and their English owners' Crusading activities.[73] Henderson recognizes that Saher's seal matrix predates his Crusading activity, although I suggest that the seal may also anticipate that activity.[74] If a viewer were to connect design 470 with the personal history of the owners of the seals that it resembled, echoes of the Crusades in this design and in this series would reverberate.

Lion Towering over a Mounted Knight

In design 469 (Figure 16), a massive lion (albeit without a mane – perhaps a lioness) towers over a mounted knight holding a sword and a shield. Here the

---

[73] Henderson, "Romance and Politics," 31.   [74] Ibid.

Figure 16 Digital reconstruction of Chertsey combat tile, lion towering over a mounted knight, and proposed reconstruction of surrounding text. Chertsey combat series tile, molds designed in the 1250s. Eames design 469. © Janis Desmarais and Amanda Luyster

focus is on the valiant steed, who both wounds and is wounded in the fight. The lion sinks its teeth into the horse's head, while the horse rears and strikes the lion with his hooves. The rearing lion and the valiant horse in design 469 share with other combat series tiles a focus on lions and additionally provide a sense of impending danger, whereas in other battles the protagonist seems to achieve easy success.

Classicizing Rider Attacked by Lion

In design 471 (Figure 17), a man clad only in a tunic turns in his saddle to deliver a deadly spear thrust, killing a lion who has reared up and buried his jaws in the rump of the man's horse. At the same time, the man grips the lion's thick mane with his left hand, and a lean hunting dog races beneath the horse's belly.

The man's ring of curls, short tunic, bare feet, and lack of stirrups suggest that this scene is based on classical or late antique iconography, probably at one or more removes from a classical source.[75] In particular, the wreath-like ring of curls was both fashionable and depicted in the fifth and sixth centuries in

---

[75] I am grateful to Ana Cabrera, Tony Cutler, and David Parks for sharing their thoughts on this design. On short tunics as classical, see Walker, *The Emperor and the World*, 26.

various locales in the late antique world.[76] Other elements of the composition, including the attacking lion and the spear-wielding mounted lion hunter, also derive from classical iconography. These Greco-Roman iconographical details may have been passed to the tile designer through the productions of post-classical cultures, including Sasanian, Islamic, or Byzantine visual traditions. Both the iconography of the front-facing attacking lion and the lance-bearing mounted lion fighter derive from traditions that date at least to classical times and can be traced through a variety of later examples, often appearing in portable objects like textiles and metalwork. The toga, for instance, can be compared to the seventh-century Byzantine David plate (Figure 11); the lack of stirrups to a fifth-century Byzantine plate in Virginia (Figure 18); and the ring of close curls about the head is repeatedly used between the fourth and sixth centuries in Sasanian metalwork (Figure 19).

This design adds in a particular way to the series of struggles between men and lions. This man's hair, clothing, and feet are distinct from those of the rest of

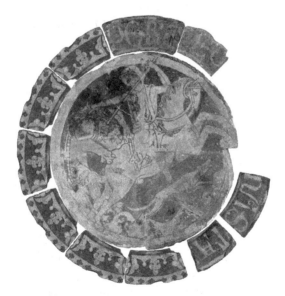

Figure 17 Physical reconstruction and restoration of Chertsey combat tile, classicizing rider attacked by a lion, and proposed reconstruction of surrounding text. Chertsey combat series tile, molds designed in the 1250s. Eames design 471. British Museum 1885,1113.9113–9120. © Janis Desmarais and Amanda Luyster

---

[76] Vida, *Late Antique Metal Vessels*, 35–36.

Figure 18 Plate depicting a man on horseback spearing a lion. Late Roman/
Byzantine, fourth or fifth century. Virginia Museum of Fine Arts, Richmond.
Adolph D. and Wilkins C. Williams Fund, 66.77. Photo: Travis Fullerton. ©
Virginia Museum of Fine Arts

the men portrayed. Some viewers would have recognized this as a classicizing
composition, an allusion to a battle from another time and place. Like the
depiction of Samson, the inclusion of this image widens the scope of
the depiction, both temporally and geographically. It encourages us to relate
the recent past, that of Richard the Lionheart, to the distant past, and to draw
whatever connections we find suitable. Some medieval or modern viewers
might associate this figure with classical horse-riding heroes, like Alexander
the Great. Alexander as a successful conqueror of lands and empire builder in
the Near East is a valuable model for Richard and Henry. However, the image
does not dictate to us that we understand it as one individual or another. Rather,
it offers us a marker in space, in the classical era, in a place where there are lions
(Greece? Syria? Asia Minor? India?), and prompts us to ask: Who might this
be? How might we compare him to Richard, to Samson? How can we understand all of these fighting men, anonymous and identified, through biblical and
classical and contemporary times, to be in dialogue with each other?

Soldiers

This section explores the iconography of the Chertsey combatants who do not
fight lions. As a group, despite their variety of clothing and equipment, all of the

Figure 19 Dish: Shapur II on a Lion Hunt. Iran, between 310 and 320. The State Hermitage Museum, St. Petersburg, Inv. No. S-253. Photo: Vladimir Terebenin. © The State Hermitage Museum

individuals included in this group may be considered soldiers, combatants who fight on behalf of a particular party or individual. In nearly all cases, they appear to fight on behalf of Richard the Lionheart. An examination of their iconography reveals the following themes: English mastery of the so-called Parthian shot (the origins of which lay in West Asia); the powerful, state-of-the-art violence of the crossbow and its association with Richard; and divine involvement, as suggested by the judicial combat.

Head of an Enemy

Eames 475 (Figure 20) contains only the head of a wounded man, a small section of the original design. Although little attention has previously been paid to this figure, he is significant, as his presence witnesses that the duel between Richard and Saladin is accompanied by other, similar Crusading combats. This man must be an enemy, as he has taken an arrow to the head and seems shocked, mouth agape. His cap resembles that of Saladin: both caps are low and sport a small hornlike projection at the top. They relate to the *pileum cornutum*, a low peaked hat often associated with Jews.[77]

---

[77] Pers. comm. David Park and Pamela Patton. See Strickland, *Saracens, Demons, and Jews*; Lipton, *Images of Intolerance*.

Figure 20 Digital reconstruction of Chertsey combat tile, head of an enemy, and proposed reconstruction of surrounding text. Chertsey combat series tile, molds designed in the 1250s. Eames design 475. © Janis Desmarais and Amanda Luyster

Despite the cap's association with Jewish figures, medieval viewers would not necessarily understand Saladin or this wounded man as Jewish. Debra Strickland describes how in medieval art the physical appearance of Jews and Muslims had many similarities.[78] In addition, correlations of hats and identities in medieval visual programs are not as consistent as we might imagine. As Sara Lipton has noted, this low, peaked type of hat in the *Bibles Moralisées* was also sometimes worn by Christians, and Jews are shown wearing this cap but also different kinds of pointed hats.[79] However, Lipton concludes that within particular compositions, despite iconographical variations, the peaked cap is frequently used as a mark of difference and as a mark of the negative qualities associated with Jews: "opposition to Christianity, fraud, unbelief, diabolical connections."[80] English manuscripts dating from the mid-thirteenth century also show low, folded peaked caps on individuals who are unconverted or evil.[81]

---

[78] Strickland, *Saracens, Demons, and Jews.*   [79] Lipton, *Images of Intolerance*, 16–19.

[80] Ibid., 19.

[81] For instance, the Lambeth Apocalypse, c. 1260–1267; the Morgan Apocalypse, ascribed to England and France between 1255 and 1260; a copy of the *Estoire d'Eracles* made in Paris c. 1295–1300.

The caps worn by Saladin and the man in 475, then, within the context of the combat series, mark them out as non-Christians, unconverted. The caps also visually associate these two men. Both men wearing caps are also the subject of violence: Saladin is run through with a lance, and this man has been shot with an arrow. Together, Saladin and the man in 475 represent the ungodly, the apostate, and the enemy, who are defeated by Christian fighters.

The Parthian Shot

Eames design 473 (Figure 21) represents a single rider, wearing a long tunic and no armor, who has just loosed an arrow from his bow. Bows played important roles in English warfare, particularly the longbow, which proved its worth during the Hundred Years' War.[82] This archer uses a bow to engage in the so-called Parthian shot. It requires the archer to remove both hands from the horse's reins and turn backwards while the horse continues running forward in a straight line, and to load and loose an arrow at the enemy behind. This is a demanding maneuver, accomplished while twisted around 180 degrees in the saddle, atop a hurtling horse.

Figure 21 Digital reconstruction of Chertsey combat tile, mounted archer turning to take the "Parthian shot," and proposed reconstruction of surrounding text. Chertsey combat series tile, molds designed in the 1250s. Eames design 473. © Janis Desmarais and Amanda Luyster

---

[82] Prestwich, *Armies and Warfare*, 131.

The Parthian shot was a well-known military technique, practiced in the era of the Crusades by both the Mamluks and the Mongols, but also in use much earlier.[83] A long-established body of iconography was also devoted to depicting its skillful execution. The Parthian Empire (247 BCE to 224 CE), from which the maneuver gains its name, was a Persian dynasty, the immediate forerunner to the Sasanian Empire (224–651 CE). The Sasanians frequently included images of the Parthian shot in royal imagery, particularly on textiles and metalwork (Figure 19).[84] By the late fifth century, Byzantine imagery, including floor mosaics at the Great Palace in Constantinople and at various other locations in Turkey, also included the Parthian shot.[85] Later Islamic textiles also included mounted archers engaged in the Parthian shot, often within roundels.[86] No doubt the visual energy of the Parthian shot, in which the rider appears coiled like a spring, in addition to its undoubted difficulty, appealed to audiences far from the Iranian heartland of the Parthian Empire. It was adopted and adapted under the Sogdians in Central Asia, at Alchi in the Himalayas (Figure 22), and in multiple textiles collected in Japanese temple treasuries.

Figure 22 Roundel showing the Parthian shot. Ceiling paintings from Alchi, Sumsteg Monastery, Ladakh (northern India). Tibetan Buddhist. Early thirteenth century. Photo: Peter van Ham

---

[83] Smith, "Ayn Jālūt: Mamlūk Sucess or Mongol Failure?," 317–318.
[84] Walker, *The Emperor and the World*, 28; Vida, *Late Antique Metal Vessels*, 28.
[85] Vida, *Late Antique Metal Vessels*, 28.   [86] Mackie, *Symbols of Power*, 49.

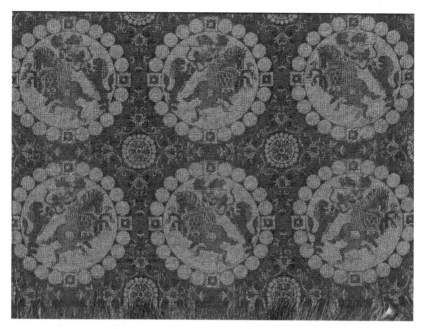

Figure 23 Reproduction of a silk twill textile, woven in Japan, imitating a Sasanian Persian original, from the Shōsō-in repository in Nara (originally held in Hōryū-ji Temple), sixth to seventh centuries. Photo: Smarthistory

An example in the Shōsō-in Treasury at Todai-ji, Nara, Japan, shows horsemen turning on their winged horses to aim their arrows at pursuing lions (Figure 23).[87] This textile seems to have been made for a Tang Chinese audience and incorporates Chinese characters, although it also relates closely to Persian iconography; it has been suggested that its manufacture was overseen by the Central Asian Sogdians.[88] Another medieval textile housed in the Hōryū-ji Temple, probably dating from the seventh or eighth century, again shows the Parthian shot in a lion-hunting scene (Figure 24).[89]

The motif of the Parthian shot traveled not only to Japan but also to the West. A Middle Byzantine ivory box shows an armored archer aiming the Parthian shot at a (rather pincushion-like) lion (Figure 25).[90] There are many other related early medieval textiles showing mounted hunters aiming arrows

---

[87] Hillenbrand, "What Happened to the Sasanian Hunt"; Hu, "Global Medieval at the 'End of the Silk Road'," 182–183.
[88] Canepa, "Textiles and Elite Tastes," 12–13.
[89] Hu, "Global Medieval at the 'End of the Silk Road'."
[90] Walker, *The Emperor and the World*.

Figure 24 Textile showing pearled roundel containing four mounted lion hunters, each engaged in the Parthian shot. Probably seventh century. Horyu-ji Temple. © Alamy

Figure 25 Imperial lion hunt, front panel of the Troyes Casket, Middle Byzantine, Constantinople (?), ivory and purple pigment, Cathedral Treasury, Troyes, France. Photo: Smarthistory

Figure 26 Amazon silk (samite). Eighth century. Found in the reliquary of the Abbaye de Faremoutiers, France. Musée Bossuet, Meaux, France. Photo: Ville de Meaux, Musée Bossuet

backward, including the so-called Amazon silks, which show mounted female archers shooting backwards (Figure 26).[91]

Even further west, the Getty's Northumberland Bestiary (Ms 100), made in England in c. 1250–1260, includes an unusual example of the Parthian shot by a man clad in a short toga, mounted on a dromedary (Figure 27).[92] The toga suggests the classical era, and the dromedary the East. Both are apt in a mid-thirteenth-century English visual reference to the Parthian shot, as the Parthians ruled during the classical era in the Near East. The Northumberland Bestiary's illustration of the Parthian shot cannot be easily compared to the manuscript's source material, since its model, a British Library bestiary made in England some fifty years earlier (Royal MS 12 C XIX, c. 1200–1210), does not contain the dromedary.[93] Intriguingly, various miniatures in the Northumberland Bestiary support the hypothesis that its artist or designer was attentive to, and knowledgeable about, geographical locations in the eastern Mediterranean and Central Asia. For instance,

---

[91] See Section 5 for further details.
[92] White, *From the Ark to the Pulpit*; Morrison, *Book of Beasts*, 98–101.
[93] Morrison, *Book of Beasts*, 100.

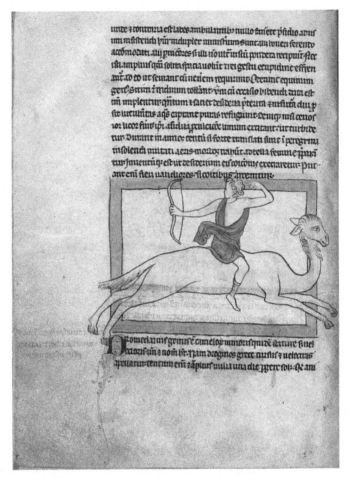

Figure 27 Northumberland Bestiary showing a dromedary, fol. 30v. England, c. 1250–1260. The J. Paul Getty Museum, Los Angeles, MS 100

while many individuals depicted in the Northumberland Bestiary, like the beaver hunter (fol. 11v), wear typical long western-style clothing, a few do not. These include the Parthian archer, who wears a toga; a man who hunts the cinnamon bird in Arabia (fol. 35v), who wears another toga; and a snake-charmer (in India?), who wears a longer but still one-shouldered costume and a turban (fol. 56r). Not every costume in the Northumberland Bestiary is dictated by geographical location, but evidence suggests that its artist is at least intermittently attentive to location-based clothing variation, attributing unusual costumes to individuals who inhabit regions in West and Central Asia.

An interest in faraway regions is also shown in the Northumberland Bestiary artist's decision to show the Parthian shot taken from the back of a dromedary. The dromedary in the Northumberland Bestiary is not described as living in any particular region, but the dromedary is a particularly swift kind of camel, and camels are said in that bestiary to be found in both Arabia and Bactria.[94] Bactria and the Parthian Empire are both parts of the historical Iranian or Persian regions of Central Asia. It is possible that the artist's addition of a tunic-wearing archer executing the Parthian shot from a speedy (Bactrian?) dromedary was a coincidence. It is also possible that the artist or designer knew that Bactria was in the same region as the ancient Parthian Empire and that the backward-facing shot was the Parthian shot. It would make sense, therefore, to add a depiction of the Parthian shot, which required speed, to a speedy creature known to live in that area.

The Northumberland artist's decision to represent the Parthian shot must have taken place at approximately the same time and place in which the designer of the Chertsey combat series made the same decision. This iconography probably had a particular currency in mid-thirteenth-century England in the context of the Crusades. A late twelfth-century wall painting (c. 1180–1190) from the crypt of Aquilea Cathedral suggests that the iconography of the Parthian shot could be associated with the Crusades, at least in Italy. In this painting, a mounted Crusader pursues a retreating Saracen, who turns on horseback to deliver the shot (Figure 28).[95] Saracen archers, as Thomas Dale notes, "were particularly noted for their abilities to attack their opponents while retreating," and were so signaled in Crusader texts.[96] Ralph of Caen's *Gesta Tancredi*, for instance, written in the first half of the twelfth century, tells of Saracen archers who "easily turn their backs, hoping, as is the custom, while fleeing to turn, and while turning to shoot": *illi* [the archers] *facile terga vertunt, sperantes, ut est moris, fugiendo gyrare, gyrando sagittare.*[97]

The visual and textual evidence from the Northumberland Bestiary, the Aquilea wall paintings, and the *Gesta Tancredi* suggest that the Parthian shot was understood in Western Europe as an attribute of West and Central Asia, associated with Bactria, the ancient Parthian Empire, and more recent Saracen forces encountered by Crusaders. The Chertsey combat tiles' representation of a European or English protagonist taking up the difficult Parthian shot, then, is probably not neutral. It shows a European or English soldier who has adopted and become proficient at a skill practiced by opposing forces in the Crusades.

---

[94] White, *From the Ark to the Pulpit*, 140–141. [95] Dale, *Relics, Prayer, and Politics*, 116–117.
[96] Ibid., 116. [97] Ibid., 116, 142, 154.

Figure 28 Crusader pursuing Saracen, Aquilea Cathedral crypt, c. 1180–1190.
Photo: Sailko, Wikimedia

While this figure is not dressed in mail, he, too, has a place in the Crusading world.

Two Crossbowmen

Eames designs 462 (Figure 29) and 468 (Figure 30) show two mounted soldiers aiming crossbows. Design 462 has sustained substantially more loss than 468, but the crossbowmen on both tiles sport long tunics over chain mail, the same clothing that Richard wears. They appear to be soldiers in his army.

The crossbows in both designs can be identified by the loop in the middle of the bow, which is part of the mechanism for drawing the bowstring. Crossbows were capable of terrible force, sufficient to pierce plate armor at appropriate range. The awe and fear inspired by the crossbow is suggested by the decision reached at the Second Lateran Council, which in 1139 forbade the use of the crossbow in battle – except against infidels, of course.[98] It does not seem that crossbows came into broad use until the late twelfth century, and even in the thirteenth century, crossbows were considered an innovative weapon in medieval England.[99] Apparently King John did not want to rely on a native Englishman to build crossbows for his forces in the early thirteenth century; he instead employed a man named Peter the Saracen.[100] We know no more

---

[98] Prestwich, *Armies and Warfare*, 129.   [99] Ibid.   [100] Ibid.

Figure 29 Digital reconstruction of Chertsey combat tile, crossbowman, and proposed reconstruction of surrounding text. Chertsey combat series tile, molds designed in the 1250s. Eames design 462. © Janis Desmarais and Amanda Luyster

Figure 30 Digital reconstruction of Chertsey combat tile, crossbowman, and proposed reconstruction of surrounding text. Chertsey combat series tile, molds designed in the 1250s. Eames design 468. © Janis Desmarais and Amanda Luyster

about Peter than his name suggests; he was presumably born (or at least spent a long time) in Muslim-ruled territories, and in these foreign lands, we may assume he learned how to build crossbows. Toward the end of the thirteenth century, Edward I only commanded about 250 English crossbowmen in his Welsh wars, although he also recruited 585 Gascon crossbowmen in 1282, most of them mounted.[101] It would have been quite difficult to operate a crossbow while riding, as the crossbow required both hands to shoot. These designs then show a powerful, innovative weapon that was regarded with awe and required highly skilled soldiers.

The crossbow was also particularly associated with Richard's Crusading endeavors. Not only was Richard supposed to be "as effective with a crossbow as with a lance," it was also well-known that his death had been brought about by an infected wound delivered by a crossbow bolt.[102] The association of Richard with the crossbow was strong enough for Matthew Paris to indicate Richard's death by means of his inverted coat of arms suspended from a crossbow.[103]

In sum, then, these two roundel designs show skilled riders, wielding weapons of serious destructive force, wearing long tunics over chain mail – just like Richard. Both men can easily be understood as well-equipped, fierce soldiers within Richard's Crusading army, and they amplify the role of the crossbow both within the Crusades and within the narrative of Richard's life.

Trial by Combat

Eames 474 (Figure 31) portrays two men, dressed alike, engaged in a duel on foot. Both men wear long tunics, sport a distinctive haircut, and grip a double-ended hammer in one hand and a square shield in the other. Both men raise their hammers and their shields; neither seems to have the advantage.

These two figures are engaged in a judicial combat, also known as a trial by combat.[104] While a relatively unusual scene, a few other medieval English examples survive. One is a (damaged) drawing underneath a painting – probably late twelfth century or early thirteenth century – of the Last Judgement and the weighing of souls in Stowell Church, Gloucestershire.[105] This drawing similarly

---

[101] Ibid., 131.

[102] Prestwich, "Richard Coeur de Lion," 15; Gillingham, "Some Legends of Richard," 53.

[103] In a manuscript of the *Chronica Majora* by Matthew Paris, fol. 85v. Thirteenth century. British Library Royal MS 14 C VII.

[104] Besson, "'A armes égales'"; Shaw, *Specimens*, 24.

[105] I am grateful to David Park of the Courtauld Institute for suggesting this and the following comparison to me. See Harvey, *Domesday: Book of Judgement*, 286; Tristram, *English Medieval Wall Painting*, 35, 45–46.

Figure 31 Digital reconstruction of Chertsey combat tile, trial by combat, and proposed reconstruction of surrounding text. Chertsey combat series tile, molds designed in the 1250s. Eames design 474. © Janis Desmarais and Amanda Luyster

shows two men on foot, armed with double-ended hammers and polygonal shields. The man on the left also has a strange haircut, in which his hair has been cropped to a vertical line above his ears. Similar iconography appears in a marginal drawing in a plea roll of 1249 (plea rolls recorded legal actions in medieval English courts of law).[106] Again, both men wield double-ended hammers, bear rectangular shields, and their hair is trimmed above their ears. Finally, the mid-thirteenth-century seal of Henry of Fernbureg, called the marshal, shows a bare-legged champion holding a rectangular shield and a narrow, pointed hammer.[107] This Henry was apparently a professional champion in trial by combat. In 1258, he "bound himself as champion to the Abbot of Glastonbury at all times against the bishop and chapter of Bath and Wells for payment of thirty marks sterling."[108] Five of those marks were to be delivered when he was shaven: *in tonsione mea quinque marcas.*[109] This explains the strange haircut. Part of the preparation for trial by combat was to be shorn, suggesting preparation for a significant ritual.[110]

---

[106] Neilson, *Trial by Combat*, 54–55; Lewis, *The Art of Matthew Paris in the Chronica Majora*, 35.
[107] Neilson, *Trial by Combat*, 54.   [108] Ibid., 53.   [109] Ibid.   [110] Ibid., 57.

The practice of trial by combat in England, introduced after the Norman Conquest, was becoming less common by the reign of Henry III, gradually being replaced by trials by jury.[111] The falling numbers of judicial combats can be traced in part by the revenues generated by and expenses associated with the Crown's participation in these trials by combat. For instance, in a single year, Henry II's coffers paid for five duels fought on the crown's behalf.[112] The crown's payments for these duels were falling off a century later, under Henry III. Still, occasional examples of crown payments to champions can be found at least through the last year of the reign of Edward I.[113] Interestingly, juridical trials were also an important part of the practice of justice in Crusader kingdoms.[114] If this trial by combat is to be understood as taking place, like the rest of the combat scenes, in the Holy Land, its practice can be historically substantiated in the medieval Crusader kingdoms. Knowledgeable viewers of the pavement would not be surprised by its presence among other events, like lion hunts, which regularly took place in the Levant.

At the time that design 474 was executed, then, trials by combat were still well known in England and in the Crusader-administered territories of the Levant. Their larger connotation would have been clear, as was signaled by the placement of the Stowell judicial combat beneath a larger image of the weighing of souls in the Last Judgement. Just as God renders judgment at the last, so too he can make his judgment clear in life by means of the trial by combat. Indeed, Crusading texts, like Robert the Monk's history of the First Crusade, attribute the Crusaders' victory to God: "Since the creation of the world what more miraculous undertaking has there been ... than what was achieved in our own time by the journey of our own people to Jerusalem? ... This was not the work of men; it was the work of God."[115] The design, in the context of the other Chertsey combats, emphasizes the role of God in choosing the rightful victor. Richard and Samson, both also represented in the Chertsey combat series, are victorious because they are chosen, and sustained, by God.

2 A Learned, Literary Composition in Latin

This section presents a reconstruction of the lost texts which originally accompanied each combat series roundel, exploring ways in which these texts contribute to the floor's representation of violence and domination. Digital tools helped to reassemble broken pieces of text and enabled new and convincing

---

[111] Ibid., 31–41.   [112] Ibid., 42.   [113] Ibid.

[114] Bishop, "Usama Ibn Munqidh and Crusader Law in the Twelfth Century," 59–61.

[115] Sweetenham, "'Hoc enim non fuit humanum opus'," 133.

readings of them. I include an interpretation of the eighty-five textual fragments in the combat series, reconstructing words and some phrases.

These Chertsey combat texts were prepared in a Latin vocabulary echoing the Vulgate and classical authors, thus adding a layer of learned sophistication to the composition. Two reconstructed phrases also suggest particular sources for the combat program, including royal seals and biblical traditions.[116] Apparently drawing from multiple sources, the combat tiles' textual program seems to be a unique composition focusing on the specific actions of battle. Many words convey the violence of certain actions – piercing, ruining, and subduing – and others focus on the weapons used to harm – the staff, claw, and spear. The violence of this language contributes to the expression of English dominance in the tile pavement.

Though the pictorial combat tiles were found alongside hundreds of fragments of tiles bearing text at the site of Chertsey Abbey, the combat series images are much better published than the texts. Our attempt is the first to treat the texts seriously. For nearly two centuries, scholars like Shaw have lamented that "it is exceedingly unfortunate" that the inscriptions are so heavily fragmented.[117] Many have worked tirelessly to reconstruct some portion of the text but, like Shaw, found it "impossible to construct a complete sentence."[118] Yet previous scholars have made some very preliminary observations which I am now able to confirm. For instance, Loomis, in 1916, detected differences in the lettering style of the Anglo-Norman (from the Tristan series) and Latin (from the combat series) inscriptions, and among the Latin words he assembled, he listed "Rex Ricardus, Leo, and Baculo."[119] Each of these words also appears in the list of words I have assembled in Table A1, although it is not certain that the name Richard was present in the nominative case (more details in the following). To Loomis, "King Richard," "lion," and "stick" suggested the inscriptions had a secular rather than a sacred content. Shaw agreed because the small number of words which he recognized seemed to have no sacred content and because none of the figures wore ecclesiastical dress. Shaw suggested that romances or chronicles might have informed their content and I will argue, based on evidence drawn from both text and image, that the combat tiles are informed by the romances and chronicles of the Crusades.

In recent years, the study of fragmentary inscriptions has undergone a quiet revolution. In cases where ink has faded or been overwritten, multispectral imaging can reveal missing letters. If a tablet or stone stele has been fragmented, digital manipulation of three-dimensional pieces can facilitate reconstruction.

---

[116] For a complete treatment of method, see Luyster, "Fragmented Tile, Fragmented Text."
[117] Shaw, *Specimens*, 23.   [118] Ibid.   [119] Loomis, *Illustrations*.

Yet the Chertsey tiles benefit from neither of these technologies. Their text is made of clay, not ink and parchment, and it remains largely legible on extant tiles. The texts were never part of a single object; instead, each mold-made segment bore a sequence of up to four letters. But the relationship of these letter sequences cannot be immediately determined. The Chertsey tiles, then, witness an unusual type of problematic fragmentary text. It is perhaps not surprising that, until the present time, scholars have not taken up the challenge of their interpretation.

The use of Latin on the combat series tiles must have been intentional, particularly given that the other well-known Chertsey series depicting Tristan bore inscriptions in Anglo-Norman.[120] Forms of French vernacular were frequently encountered in accounts of the Crusades by the thirteenth century, by which time both of the dominant accounts of the Crusade (the prose *Eracles* and the Old French Crusade Cycle) were in Old French.[121] By contrast, the choice of Latin for the combat tiles suggests a connection to learning and to biblical history; it implies a particular status and a select audience for its narrative.[122] The Latin vocabulary used in the series words would have seemed familiar to readers from the Vulgate. Forms of ACCIDIT, PERIT, BACULO, AUDET, UNGUE, TEGO, and VIRTUS each appear more than fifteen times in the Vulgate; some appear more than 300 times.[123] Furthermore, some of the vocabulary used on the tiles is unusually sophisticated and high-flown, reminiscent of first- and second-century Roman authors like Lucan, Statius, and Virgil.[124] Lucan, for example, was quoted a number of times in a Crusade context in Robert the Monk's early twelfth-century *Historia Iherosolimitana*.[125]

In literature, it is not difficult to find the presentation of Crusading heroes, including Richard the Lionheart, alongside other heroes. The poet Joseph of Exeter composed an original Latin text on the First Crusade c. 1190, and the surviving lines include allusions to Troy, Rome, and Arthur.[126] Ambroise, the Norman chronicler who followed Richard I on the Third Crusade, wrote about his experience in Old French after his return (after 1195). Ambroise described the landscape through which Richard moved as marked by biblical history and also compared the heroes of the Crusade, including

---

[120] Ibid., 24; Eames, *Catalogue*, 1: 144.   [121] Carol Sweetenham, pers. comm., July 2019.

[122] I have benefitted greatly here from discussions with Carol Sweetenham. See also Sweetenham and Paterson, *The Canso d'Antioca*.

[123] According to the Tufts Perseus Word Frequency tool: www.perseus.tufts.edu/hopper/wordfreq?lookup=accidit&lang=la&sort=max.

[124] Carol Sweetenham, pers. comm., July 2019.

[125] Carol Sweetenham, pers. comm., June 2018.

[126] Carol Sweetenham, pers. comm., July 2019.

Richard, to heroes like Hector, Achilles, Alexander, and Arthur.[127] The Middle English *Richard Coer de Lyon*, which developed from an early version created probably in the late thirteenth century, centered on the deeds of Richard in the Third Crusade and contained allusions to a wide variety of heroes including classical figures, like Hercules; epic characters, like Alexander and Charlemagne; and Arthurian models.[128] These juxtapositions between Crusading heroes like Richard and other heroes enabled listeners – and, in the case of the Chertsey tiles, viewers – to participate in an apparently never-ending discussion comparing a multitude of heroes and their great deeds.

Summary of Conclusions Regarding the Inscriptions

The tiles bearing sequences of letters survive in eighty-five designs. The relevant tile fragments are nearly all housed, like most of the pictorial fragments, at the British Museum.[129] The text tiles are mostly complete, but there are a small number of broken and therefore incomplete tiles. Each sequence of letters, complete or incomplete, is between one and four characters in length; for example, IA, FRE, RICA, and so on. Many tiles also include punctuation, abbreviations, and ligatures. The collection of eighty-five designs is almost certainly incomplete; it seems highly unlikely that all of the text designs originally made have come down to us, some 750 years later. What we have is certainly not the entire original text; nor can we be certain what percentage of the original whole we now retain.

In Table A1, I list words which I consider highly likely to have been part of the original Chertsey combat inscriptions, listed alphabetically according to the extant text fragments. The reconstructed vocabulary in this list is generally violent. Of nine reconstructed verbs, eight clearly relate to the actions of war: *growing in power/violence, daring, raising/exalting, piercing, breaking/subduing, perishing, ruining,* and *defending.* Among the reconstructed nouns, some refer to the subjects depicted, including *lion, king,* and *knight,* as well as concepts that are not depicted but which can be understood as implied, like *death, wars,* and *victory.* There are proper names, like Richard and Samson. However, there is also a group of words that describe the means by which military actions were undertaken. These include *by the staff, by claw/talon,* and *by the spear.* The visceral nature of much of the reconstructed vocabulary focuses the reader's attention on the bloody, physical, and forceful effort of

---

[127] Prestwich, "Richard Coeur de Lion," 3.   [128] Carol Sweetenham, pers. comm., July 2019.
[129] For accession numbers, see Table B in Luyster, "Fragmented Tile, Fragmented Text."

war. Its eventual success – *victory* – is also emphasized in the vocabulary of the inscription.

Finally, an attempt was made to connect these words into phrases, in relationship to the image roundels. This attempt should be understood as exploratory and hypothetical rather than prescriptive and definitive. There is no physical evidence sequencing any of these words or, indeed, word fragments in a particular order. However, the Chertsey inscriptions did originally appear as phrases around the image roundels, and it behooves us to attempt to put the pieces back together. Some progress can be made by examining the list of likely words and determining whether any of those words have long-standing connections with any of the named figures represented on the tiles.

The inscriptions surrounding Richard and Samson can be reconstructed with a reasonable degree of accuracy because they depict an identifiable subject that has historically been associated with particular words and phrases. When we move instead to associate words with other roundels, these associations must remain more hypothetical. Yet these attempts retain scholarly value as a broad-brush rendering: the Chertsey roundels, when intact and surrounded by text, probably looked and functioned "something like" the reconstructions we suggest.

Richard the Lionheart (466)

The tile showing Richard is one of the two combat designs that can be convincingly linked to specific surrounding text. In order to reconstruct the text that originally surrounded this roundel of Richard, we consult the list of words from Table A1 designated highly likely to be present in the Chertsey inscription, and we also look for other inscriptions which were frequently used in conjunction with images of Richard. For instance, Richard's first Great Seal bore the text *RICARDUS DEI GRACIA REX ANGLORUM*, and his second Great Seal styled him similarly, *RICARDUS DEI GRATIA REX ANGLORUM*.[130] Two "highly likely" words from Table A1, GRA/TIA (*by grace of*) and REX (*king*), thereby have a customary connection with the title of the English king. Also in Table A1 we find RICA[rdus] and AN/GLI. We therefore have tile text segments from Chertsey that could have been connected as following (Figure 4); capital letters are used for extant tiles, lower case letters are used for suggested lost letters, and the / symbol denotes a break between tile segments):

---

[130] Wyon and Wyon, *Great Seals*, 18–19.

RICA/rdus/ dei/ GRAT/IA:/ REX/ AN/GLIe

Richard, by grace of God, the King of England

Note that ANG/LI (for AN/GLIe) appears in the tile fragments rather than ANGLORUM. Under Richard's brother and successor, King John, the regnal title was changed slightly to replace *Anglorum* with *Anglie*, yielding *JOHANNES DEI GRACIA REX ANGLIE DOMINUS HIBERNIE*;[131] that is, King of England rather than King of the English. John's son was Henry III, who ruled during the time of the Chertsey tiles' commission, and who may have commissioned the tiles for Westminster Palace. Both Henry's first and second Great Seals include the phrase *HENRICUS DEI GRATIA REX ANGLIE*.[132] Therefore, it seems probable that the image of Richard was surrounded by tile fragments spelling out some version of his regnal title.

Samson (472)

This design is the second one (in addition to that depicting Richard the Lionheart) for which we have comparative data to inform a reconstruction of the original accompanying inscription. The name Samson is attested on a Chertsey text tile in an abbreviated form that makes it difficult to know its case (~SAM): for this reason, the name SAMSON has long been recognized as present in some form in these tiles. Table A1 also presents the words ORA (jaws) and LEO (lion), which relate to the roundel depicting Samson rending the jaws of the lion. Table A1 additionally contains two other words, FOR/TIS and VIRTUS, which are also frequently used in reference to Samson, although they are not part of the Vulgate text in which Samson appears. Samson's story appeared in many commentaries and gave rise to a substantial visual tradition, to which the Chertsey tile roundel belongs, which is also witnessed on objects as varied as church capitals and ivory game pieces.[133] In addition, the use of Samson as a type for Christ, and his foe, the lion, as a type for the devil, has been widely recognized.[134]

From Table A1, we now have five words with substantiated connections to the roundel depicting Samson and the lion. These are SAM[son], LEO, ORA, FOR/TIS, and VIRTus. If all of these words relate to this roundel, we next need to decide how to order and connect them. Later copies of Chertsey text tiles have additional information which is relevant here (Figure 32). A reconstruction that

---

[131] Ibid., 20.   [132] The second Great Seal bears "*Gracia*" instead of "*Gratia*." Ibid., 21–22.
[133] Luyster, "Fragmented Tile, Fragmented Text," 104–109.
[134] Ambrose, "Samson, David, or Hercules," 2.

Figure 32 Tile showing text from Chertsey combat mosaic and a section of the Samson design. CHYMS.2000.008. © The Chertsey Museum

takes into account all words connected to Samson and the ordering witnessed in these tiles from the second series is as follows (Figure 9, the capital letters refer to extant tiles; the lower case letters are proposed reconstructions; the capital letters in italics refer to the expanded form of contractions present on the tiles):

+ VIRT*US*/ SAM*SONIS*/ FOR/TIS/ FRE/git/ ORA/ LEO/NIS

The courage of Samson the Strong broke the jaws of the lion.

Saladin (467)

Scholars have long recognized the presence of Saladin on these tiles (Figure 5). It may be that Saladin was surrounded by text bearing a variant of his name: SEL/LIA/DEN. If not part of Saladin's name, the fragment SEL is otherwise difficult to explain. SEL is not common in frequency dictionaries. The Latin word that SEL most commonly appears in is "sella," or chair. There are no chairs depicted on the roundels. In addition, other text fragments are present – LIA and DEN – that could have conjoined to create the name SEL/LIA/DEN, a variant of the name Saladin. The Arabic Salah ad-Din, habitually transliterated into English as Saladin, might also have been transliterated as Salahuddin, Salaheddine, or numerous other variants in use today.[135] William of Tyre, in

---

[135] See, for instance, the Wikipedia page devoted to "Salah ad-Din (name)" at https://en.wikipedia .org/wiki/Salah_ad-Din_(name).

his Latin chronicle, uses *Salahadinus*.[136] If we ignore the presence of the letter H, which is unvoiced, and William of Tyre's use of a final S to create a Latin nominative, then the tile combination SEL/LIA/DEN contains the same consonants in the same order as Salah ad-Din, Salahuddin, Salaheddine, and Salahadinus: S – L – D – N.

Three other text fragments could also have been placed around design 467. The fragment containing the abbreviation :Ro seems suggestive. The colon signals that this is the beginning of a word; the word begins with R and, as suggested by the vertical ascender on the R, letters have been omitted. The word either ends with O or contains a significant O. It is a reasonable assumption that in this series, in which Richard plays a prominent role, and in which Saladin is clearly wounded by Richard, that :Ro could mean "by Richard" and would have been placed around design 467. We would then expect a verb. The fragment FIGI would work well here. FIGI is present in two common words, *figo* and *effigies*. We have the tile pieces to make FIGI/TUR, or "is pierced," which is a word also witnessed in Crusading texts. The movement of the lance through Saladin's body could certainly be described as "piercing." Therefore, the inscription around this design could have read, using extant fragments, SEL/LIA/DEN/:Ro/FIGI/TUR: "Saladin is pierced by Richard."

Head of an Enemy (475)

Other than Saladin, there is only one other design that depicts an enemy combatant: design 475. It is possible that at least four text fragments encircled this roundel. The abbreviated fragment C#Ri should be expanded as C'RERI or C'RARI. This may be a form of *contrarius*, meaning opponent, enemy, or hostile, which could make sense around this roundel. We also have two other fragments that could fit here: MORS, a complete and common word ("death"), and ACCI/DIT. An inscription around this roundel could have read, using extant fragments, MORS/C#Ri/ACCI/DIT, "The death of the enemy comes to pass."

Two Crossbowmen and an Archer (the Parthian Shot) (462, 468, 473)

It is difficult to associate any of these roundels with specific text. There are plenty of text options that would make sense, including O:MI/LES, HIC BEL/LA, :GLI/SCO, or Vict/ORIA:/ELA/ti ("the knight," "here are wars," "I rise in

---

[136] William of Tyre, *Historia Rerum In Partibus Transmarinis Gestarum*, LIBER XX, CAPUT XII. www.thelatinlibrary.com/williamtyre/20.html#8.

power/violence," or "having been raised up by [their] victory"). The last phrase in particular, "having been raised up by [their] victory," seems convincing as a part of the program somewhere. It is witnessed in at least one other medieval Latin text, William of Tyre's *A History of Deeds Done Beyond the Sea* (written between 1170 and 1184), as well as in classical texts, for instance the commentaries on the Gallic and Alexandrine wars by Julius Caesar.[137] These three roundels might then have been surrounded by text mentioning knights, the wars, growing in power or violence, or being raised up by victory.

Trial by Combat (474)

Many of the reconstructed words and phrases refer to weapons or actions not present in this trial by combat. For instance, knights, enemies, and piercing all make less sense here, as no knights, no clear enemy, and no piercing are present. One word that would work is TEG/O:, meaning "I protect or defend."

Man Raising Club (463)

BAC/ULO, "by the stick," was one of the few words recognized by earlier scholars. That word seems to make most sense in conjunction with this roundel. All of the other roundels show individuals using lances, swords, and arrows; even the trial by combat shows hammers. This is the only roundel in which a stick-like object is used, and *baculi* appears in the text of the Vulgate as hitting-sticks; see Isaiah 10.24. The second-person verb RUIS could have been used here as well, yielding (with extant fragments) RUIS/BAC/ULO, "You destroy by means of a stick."

Lion and Standing Knight (470)

The claws of the lion against the knight's shield are a particular iconographical signifier, playing a role in romances, as already noted. The fragment GUE: is a distinctive ending, with only three words seeming possible according to frequency dictionaries (*pingue*, *angue*, and *ungue*); of these, UN/GUE: ("by

---

[137] "Videtur ergo mihi quod hostes de praesenti aliquantulum **elati victoria**, imprudentius se habebunt; et de sua virtute praesumentes, per nos ad urbem redire, praedam et manubias inferre non verebuntur." William of Tyre, *Historia Rerum In Partibus Transmarinis Gestarum*, Liber Quintus, Caput V. www.thelatinlibrary.com/williamtyre/5.html.

"At nostri **victoria elati** subire iniquum locum munitionesque aggredi non dubitarunt." Julius Caesar (attrib.), *De Bello Alexandrino*, 76.2. www.thelatinlibrary.com/caesar/alex.shtml.

"At nostri equites, qui paulo ante cum resistentibus fortissime conflixerant, laetitia **victoriae elati** magno undique clamore sublato cedentibus circumfusi, quantum equorum vires ad persequendum dextraeque ad caedendum valent, tantum eo proelio interficiunt." Julius Caesar [Aulus Hirtius], *Commentarii de Bello Gallico*, 8.29.3. www.thelatinlibrary.com/caesar/gall8.shtml#29.

claw") makes the most sense with the extant roundels. We also have fragments AUD/ET:/VUL/NERE, "he dares to wound," which would focus attention, appropriately, on the lion and his violent character, threatening the knight. Using extant fragments, this inscription could read AUD/ET:/VUL/NERE/ UN/GUE, "He dares to wound by means of a claw."

Lion Towering over Mounted Knight (469)

Fragments remain that can create the relatively common past participle, PE/ NET/RATUS ("having been penetrated"). The grammatical form means that the subject needs to be being penetrated, so the subject needs to be someone other than one of the knights (who are not wounded). The fragment LEO works here. It is possible that other fragments, LEO and MAGNUS, surrounded this roundel to yield MAGN/us/LEO/PE/NET/RATUS, "The great lion, having been penetrated."

Classicizing Rider Attacked by Lion (471)

The fragment HAS could reasonably be interpreted as a plural accusative pronoun: "these"; or with the fragment TA to form HAS/TA, either a nominative or ablative form of "spear." If it is interpreted as HAS/TA, then it could refer only to the battle between Richard and Saladin or this roundel, as these are the only roundels present in which a spear is used. The genitive MILITIS is found in the second series tiles, and LEO:M is also found in the second series tiles. If these fragments were used together, LEO needs to be nominative, MILITIS is genitive, and we need a verb. PERIT would work. The roundel could then have been accompanied by the inscription, PERIT/ LEO/:MILITIS/HAS/TA:, "The lion perishes by means of the spear of the knight." Lions, knights, spears, and victims perishing can all be found on other roundels. Still, this reading does at least have the advantage of being grammatically correct, relying only on extant fragments, accurately describing the scene on the roundel, and incorporating evidence provided by two second series tiles.

Reassembling Fragments: Valiant Combats in the Holy Land

The reconstruction of word fragments provides a set of useful conclusions. These include the visceral violence of much of the included vocabulary, focusing on weapons and military acts of wounding, killing, and achieving victory. The reconstruction of phrases surrounding Richard the Lionheart and Samson the Strong suggests that the program's designer looked to a variety of sources in order to create an original program.

The effect of a juxtaposition between Samson and Richard, two mighty fighters, would, I suggest, heighten the viewer's sense of Richard's physical strength, courage, and divine backing. These seem all the more true when we recognize that both of their foes are types of Satan. Samson's lion is frequently interpreted as a figure of the devil, as already discussed. Richard's opponent in battle, Saladin, can similarly be recognized as an unchristian apostate. On the Chertsey tiles, both the English king and the biblical hero then engage in violent struggle in the Holy Land against ungodly figures. Richard and Samson show forth both their physical power and their courage. Their followers depicted in the remaining roundels, knights and combatants of many kinds, are inspired by their example and fight ever more valiantly. Small wonder that, in the end, they are raised up by victory – Vict/ORIA:/ELA/ti.

3 Findspots: Chertsey Abbey and Winchester Cathedral

Ceramics, like textiles, could travel far from their sites of manufacture. Fragments of Chinese vessels are regularly discovered on the coast of east Africa; medieval English ceramic jugs were found in a courtyard in West Africa; pieces of Islamic bowls appear in excavations of medieval English sites.[138] The Chertsey tiles, however, may not have traveled far. The Chertsey tiles were made using sets of wooden or metal molds, and it is likely that the Chertsey tile *molds* – rather than the *tiles* – were later carried to other locations after their initial commission at Westminster. The tiles we have today were unearthed at two sites: Chertsey Abbey, some twenty miles southwest of London, and Winchester Cathedral, fifty miles farther in the same direction. A kiln was excavated on the grounds of Chertsey Abbey; this kiln and adjacent wasters strongly suggest that tiles were made on site for Chertsey Abbey.[139] No evidence remains to suggest how or why the tile molds ended up at either Chertsey or Winchester. Tile molds could have been carried by one or more craftsmen across the country as one job finished and another began.[140] This section treats the two findspots in which the Chertsey tiles have been found, connecting each findspot to its historical and spatial context, paying particular attention to the movement of objects and individuals.

---

138 For an introduction to ceramics, textiles, and other media moving to and from medieval England, see the series of recorded public lectures entitled "Britain and the World," Yale University's Paul Mellon Centre for Studies in British Art, London, UK. Recorded in spring 2022 and available online.
139 Eames and Gardner, "A Tile Kiln at Chertsey Abbey."
140 Betts, *Medieval "Westminster" Floor Tiles*, 16.

The unusually large chapter house at Chertsey Abbey and its similarly sized adjacent room may be understood at least partly in the light of the chapter house's function as a social space intended for lay and ecclesiastical visitors. In this commission, Chertsey takes its place alongside other thirteenth-century religious foundations in England, many of whom were constructing architecture either particularly designed for or well-suited to hospitality. Chertsey Abbey lay not only along the Thames but also near one of the major roads leading from London. Its position enabled it to act as a stopping place for travelers, royal and otherwise, who moved around the country along its major waterways and roads. The use of the Chertsey tiles at Winchester Cathedral was likely in association with a special commission for a particular altar, perhaps the altar of St. Swithun, and should be viewed in association with the possible use of Chertsey combat tiles at Winchester Castle.

Chertsey Abbey's Chapter House

In 1988, the archaeologist Rob Poulton identified Chertsey Abbey's chapter house, originally uncovered in 1855 but misidentified as the south transept of the church, as the main location where the great majority of the Chertsey roundels had been found in the nineteenth century (Figure 33).[141] Hence, this group of tiles is called Chertsey tiles; however, as we will see, not all examples of these tiles were discovered or used at Chertsey. Poulton notes that the tiles were not in situ, and the floor had evidently been broken up.[142] Beneath the mortar bed containing the tiles, a number of stone and wooden coffins were excavated; these presumably contained the bodies of the abbots.[143] While very little remains of Chertsey Abbey or its chapter house, we have worked with Chertsey Museum to create a digital recon-struction of Chertsey's chapter house, including an artist's rendering of the combat tiles, as well as the zodiac and Tristan series, laid in the pavement of the chapter house (Figure 34).[144] While no information remains as to how any of these tiles were actually laid, we drew inspiration from surviv-ing tiled floors in medieval England in order to imagine the original appearance of the entire pavement.

In addition to the large pile of tiles found in the chapter house, one additional fragment of a combat roundel was found in another region of the abbey. This

---

[141] Poulton, *Archaeological Investigations*, 33.   [142] Ibid.   [143] Ibid.
[144] We are grateful to Emma Warren at the Chertsey Museum and James Cumper for partnering with us in this project. Full results available at https://youtu.be/ibES5UxGJkk.

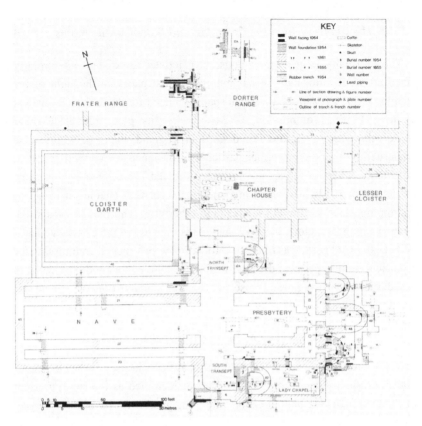

Figure 33 Plan of Chertsey Abbey, showing chapter house, coffins, and mass of broken tiles in center. Reproduced courtesy of Rob Poulton and Surrey Archaeological Society

Figure 34 Digital reconstruction of the interior of Chertsey Abbey's chapter house, including the combat series tiles. Still from a 3D flythrough created by James Cumper and the Chertsey Museum, available at https://youtu.be/ibES5UxGJkk

fragment, depicting Saladin, was recovered in 1954, although its precise location was not included in Poulton's publication.[145] As the locations of the 1954 trenches were focused on (although not limited to) the east end of the church, however, it is possible that the Saladin fragment was found in the church's east end.[146] Still, none of the fragments of the combat roundels were found in situ, and the site has been much disturbed from the time of the Dissolution and onward. Therefore, it seems probable that the combat roundels were laid in the chapter house, where the large pile was found, and perhaps elsewhere in the church.

Poulton has reasonably suggested that a fire in 1235 instigated new work on the church's east end and surrounding areas, and that this provided the context for the integration of Chertsey tiles into the abbey's pavements. The new work on the abbey's east end may have carried on into the late thirteenth century.[147] Certainly the apsed chapels at the church's east end were adapted to a square plan at some point.[148] In addition, the stiff leaf sculptured capitals of the lady chapel (Figure 35) have been dated stylistically to the 1250s or 1260s and have been compared to sculpture in the chapter house at Westminster.[149] The comparison of Chertsey's sculpted capitals from the 1250s and 1260s to coeval work at Westminster makes it less surprising to see tilework with formal links to work at Westminster also being laid at Chertsey, also in a similar time period.

The chapter house at Chertsey was extremely large, measuring 88 feet long by 39 feet wide.[150] It was also accompanied by another room just to the north which had similar dimensions. The function of the second room is not clear; it may have been a parlor or warming room.[151] The size of the Chertsey chapter house is almost unprecedented in English monastic history, and its "twinning" with a room of similar size makes one suspect that such a chamber was built with aspirational aims.

Chertsey's geographical location contributed to regular contact between its abbot, the crown, and other significant individuals in medieval England. The abbey was founded in 666 as a Benedictine house, devoted to St. Peter.[152] It rose only half a mile from the Thames River, and a smaller waterway either dug or expanded by the monks, today known as Abbey River, brought boats practically to the doors of the abbey itself. The Thames was a well-worn medieval "road," enabling easy transportation between

---

[145] Poulton, *Archaeological Investigations*, 49.   [146] Ibid., 60.   [147] Ibid., vii, 4, 31, 81.
[148] Ibid., 31, 81.   [149] Williamson, "Capitals from Chertsey Abbey."
[150] Poulton, *Archaeological Investigations*, 33.   [151] Ibid.   [152] Ibid.

Figure 35 Capitals and fragments in Purbeck marble found in the excavations of the chapter house, Chertsey Abbey, September 1861. Photo: M. Shurlock, SyAS Res Collections 55/1/6. Reproduced with kind permission of the Surrey Archaeological Society and Surrey History Centre. © Surrey Archaeological Society

London and the West Country. Chertsey Abbey's position along this waterway must have led to increased interaction with people and goods, and the abbey could have been originally sited at this position partly for its proximity to a major river. Still, not all traffic went by river. The main Roman road leading west from London (the Portway) passed through Staines-upon-Thames, only three miles to the north of Chertsey, and it was at that very point that the Roman road crossed the Thames.[153]

Itineraries witness that Henry III – and presumably Eleanor of Provence, although records following her travels are more difficult to reconstruct – was a relatively frequent guest at Chertsey.[154] Often, Henry stayed at Chertsey while journeying between Westminster and Windsor. And when Henry and Eleanor traveled to the Thames Valley/Wessex, many others – not only their households but also any other local, national, or international figures who wished to meet with them – traveled there, too. The role of the Thames Valley/Wessex region

---

[153] Harrison, *The Bridges of Medieval England*, 21–22, 55, 69.
[154] Craib, *The Itinerary of Henry III*, 27–72.

remained significant in later years, when Edward I, II, and III also stayed at Chertsey.[155]

The unusually large chapter house at Chertsey Abbey, and the sizeable adjacent room, functioned as social spaces intended for lay and ecclesiastical visitors as well as for the local monastic community. Monasteries used chapter houses for regular chapter practice, including readings and sermons, to receive postulants, and to hear important announcements.[156] However, chapter houses were also associated with the "corporate aspects of monastic foundations."[157] At Norton priory in the mid-thirteenth century, the chapter house was the space in which legal contracts were agreed, at least at times, in person.[158] And in addition to corporate activities, as Peter Fergusson has explained, many monasteries focused on the practice of hospitality, and chapter houses were specifically used to welcome visitors.[159] Visitors with their own business to conduct, including the king and bishops, would also very likely conduct that business from the chapter house. Therefore, the abbot of Chertsey could well have had it in mind to impress elite visitors with a particularly large and beautifully floored chapter house, within which meetings would be held and business attended to. The chapter house pavement contained tiles from multiple pictorial series, but the Crusades-themed combat series would have been particularly suitable for visitors, lay or ecclesiastical, who were setting out on or returning from Crusade. As pointed out by Nicholas Paul, chapter houses often served as the site for ceremonial leave-takings and returns from Crusade.[160]

The decision to pave the chapter house and other spaces at Chertsey with such unusual tiles was probably made or at least approved by the abbot of Chertsey. The date at which the combat tiles were first laid at Chertsey is, however, unknown. Previous scholars have generally located this date as after 1250, the presumed date of the tiles' commission, and before 1307. The latter date coincides with the beginning of John de Rutherwyk's tenure as abbot. Records of the years under John de Rutherwyk's abbotship are rich and, it has been argued, the operation of a tile kiln would have left some trace in his financial records – and as no record remains, the tile kiln was presumably no longer in use by 1307. The period c. 1250–1307 at Chertsey intersects with the tenures of three abbots: Alan, 1223–1261, who was one of the signators of the

[155] Toms, *Chertsey Abbey Court Rolls Abstract*, viii; Crockford, "The Itinerary of Edward I," 245.
[156] Fergusson and Harrison, *Rievaulx Abbey*, 95.   [157] Gilyard-Beer, "Byland Abbey," 65.
[158] Greene, *Medieval Monasteries*, 9.
[159] Fergusson et al., *Rievaulx Abbey*, 95; Fergusson, "Canterbury Cathedral Priory's Bath House."
[160] Lecture given by Nicholas Paul, Fordham University, entitled *Paving Over Paradise: The Aristocratic Landscape and the Crusading Experience, 1187–1291* at the College of the Holy Cross, March 25, 2023. www.youtube.com/watch?v=ofbUXHXrtQg.

reissue of the Magna Carta; John de Medmenham, 1261–1272; and Bartholomew de Winchester, 1272–1307.[161] Unfortunately no evidence has survived to link the installation of the tiles to the tenure of any particular abbot.

Chertsey Combat Tiles at Winchester Cathedral

For more than a century, the only site at which the combat roundels had been found was Chertsey Abbey. In 1971, however, Mr. Carpenter Turner discovered some unusually shaped tile fragments in the rubble under the steps leading up to the presbytery at Winchester Cathedral. He brought them to Elizabeth Eames, who identified them as part of the series of Chertsey combat roundels. Three designs from the combat series were discovered in the rubble: the trial by combat, Samson, and one additional design that is worn and difficult to identify.[162] Later an additional combat fragment was discovered at Winchester Cathedral in the same general area, this time in a trench under the choir stalls. All of the combat tile fragments were heavily worn, suggesting that they had been in an area which had seen high traffic.

The location in which the combat tiles were discovered at Winchester Cathedral suggests, as Christopher Norton has written, that they were probably laid in the presbytery.[163] They were unlike the rest of the tiles used in that area, which were of the Wessex type, and hence were probably brought in as part of a special commission for a specific area of floor. Norton suggests that they could have been laid near the high altar or perhaps in front of the tomb of St. Swithin, which may have been being reworked in the mid-thirteenth century.[164] Norton writes that the combat roundels were probably laid when the rest of the presbytery was being tiled, c. 1260.[165]

The discovery of the combat roundels at Winchester Cathedral yields three conclusions. First, the combat tiles were not just used at Chertsey; they were used in at least one other location. Indeed, more combat roundels could be preserved elsewhere, unrecognized. Second, there were plenty of tile designs (from the Wessex group) already in use at Winchester Cathedral. Therefore, a special decision must have been made to bring the combat roundels in – these were highly regarded tiles; somebody specifically wanted them in a certain location at Winchester Cathedral. And, third, nearly all of the Wessex designs laid in the east end of Winchester Cathedral were also used at Winchester

---

[161] Surrey Record Society, *Chertsey Abbey Cartularies*, ix.

[162] Norton, "The Medieval Tile Pavements of Winchester Cathedral," 80. See also the later publication by the same author under an identical title: Norton, "The Medieval Tile Pavements of Winchester Cathedral," 171.

[163] Norton, "The Medieval Tile Pavements of Winchester Cathedral," 80.   [164] Ibid.

[165] Ibid.

Castle. This strong connection between designs used at Winchester Cathedral and Winchester Castle suggests that the combat tiles might also have been used at that palace. We will return to this hypothesis, as it can also be supported with another body of evidence.

4 Commission: Westminster Palace

This section opens with a brief survey of the use of glazed figural tiles in other locations around the medieval world, especially in Ilkhanid Iran, which contain comparable iconography to that of the Chertsey tiles. It then focuses on the circumstances of the Chertsey tiles' commission at Westminster Palace and explores the possibility of their patronage by Eleanor of Provence for her "Antioch chamber," a room dedicated to Crusading themes.

Medieval palaces and shrines around the world relied on tiled decoration on floors and walls to enhance their grandeur. Relatively inexpensive and generally durable, glazed tiles were both showy and practical. While the technique used to create the Chertsey tiles arose in France, tiles made much farther away also share similarities in theme and iconography. For instance, thirteenth-century lusterware tiles, with their iridescent shimmer, made for the Ilkhanid palace at Takht-i Soleymän in Iran, also bore images of horsemen and combats with beasts (Figure 36). Indeed, another Iranian glazed tile, made either in the

Figure 36 Frieze tile with two hunters. Attributed to Iran, Kashan, second half of the thirteenth century. Gift of George Blumenthal, 1910. Metropolitan Museum of Art, 10.9.1

Figure 37 Frieze tile showing two hunters, one engaged in the Parthian shot. Attributed to Iran, thirteenth or fourteenth century. Staatliche Museen zu Berlin, Museum für Islamische Kunst/Christian Krug CC BY-SA 4.0

thirteenth or fourteenth century, includes an image of the Parthian shot (Figure 37). While it is not my aim to argue that the Chertsey tiles or this Iranian tile had any direct impact on each other, both grew from larger, global interests in the potential for figural tile décor and the way in which tile molds could be used to create combat imagery, including the in-vogue Parthian shot.

In this section, I associate the commission of the Chertsey combat tiles (for which we have the objects but no documented original context) with the commission of the royal Antioch chambers (which provide a documented context but no known objects). I outline the likelihood that Eleanor of Provence, who commissioned the first Antioch chamber (showing events of the Crusades, including the battle of Antioch) at Westminster Palace, was the original patron of the Chertsey combat tiles. This commission was probably made in association with Henry and Eleanor's March 1250 vow to go on Crusade. In this connection, one candidate for the Chertsey tile texts' author is a Latin poet with whom Eleanor had contact; he is known to have written a poem which included Crusaders.

Westminster and the History of Inlaid Tiles in England

In the early twentieth century, the architect, scholar, and surveyor of Westminster Abbey W. R. Lethaby described a connection in technique, subject, and style between the Chertsey tiles and a group of tiles in Westminster Abbey's chapter house.[166] Over many decades, other scholars, including Elizabeth Eames, the editors of the *Age of Chivalry* catalogue, and Christopher Norton, have echoed this association, repeatedly suggesting, due to similarities in technique, subject, and style, that the molds for the combat tiles used at Chertsey were likely originally a royal commission for Westminster Palace. However, no remains of the combat tiles have ever been discovered at Westminster Abbey or Westminster Palace.

Both the combat tiles and the relevant Westminster chapter house tiles bear formal similarities in subject and style. While a variety of tiles is used in the Westminster chapter house, a group showing secular subject matter stands out. These may have been left over from a paving project elsewhere in the palace.[167] The tiles are simple squares; they do not have the combat tiles' complex mosaic layout or surrounding text. However, they show unusual figural motifs that are more sophisticated than is the norm in tiled floors. The designs include two musicians, an abbot, a three-tile hunting scene, King Edward the Confessor giving his ring to a pilgrim, a queen, and a king (Figure 38).[168] Thirteenth-century floor tiles were much more commonly simpler ornamental motifs like

Figure 38 Tile showing a hunter in the chapter house, Westminster Abbey, London. Pavement laid in the 1250s. Photo: Author

---

[166] Lethaby, "Romance Tiles," 78; Lethaby, *Westminster Abbey Re-Examined*, 113.
[167] Eames, *English Medieval Tiles*, 43.   [168] Ibid., 1: 43; Norton, "The Luxury Pavement," 21.

rosettes, or heraldic motifs, or lions in circles. Lethaby pointed to the drawing style and rendering of drapery, particularly in the images of kings and huntsmen, as closely comparable with the Chertsey tiles.[169] The unusual subject matter and careful drawing of the secular motifs of the Westminster chapter house tiles provide the closest extant parallel to the combat series tiles found at Chertsey.

The date at which the combat tile molds were commissioned, presumably although not definitively at Westminster, is unknown, but scholarly consensus rests on the 1250s.[170] The dates of the secular-themed Westminster chapter house tiles provide a reference point for the commission of the Chertsey combat molds. The chapter house at Westminster Abbey was completed by 1258/1259, at which date Henry ordered that tiles surplus from that project should be laid elsewhere in the Abbey.[171] But work had been going on in the chapter house for some time; Henry's lectern for that space had been commissioned in 1249 and its completion and transfer to the chapter house in May 1256 suggests that by that date, if not before, the chapter house floor was complete and ready for use.[172] Even before that, however, in 1253, canvas was ordered to cover the chapter house windows, suggesting that the space was nearly complete and that some use was being made of it.[173] The floor tiles would have been among the last additions to the space before it was brought into use.

The broader context of the use of inlaid tiles in the British Isles should also be taken into account when considering a date for the commission of the combat molds. The use of two-color inlaid tiles seems to have developed in France sometime before 1240, and they then appear in England "almost overnight" in high-status ecclesiastical environments and elite residences.[174] In the early 1240s, Winchester Cathedral and Salisbury Cathedral commissioned two-color pavements. These seem to have been made by the same workshop which also provided tiles to Henry III in the 1240s, including at Winchester Castle and Clarendon Palace.[175] Christopher Norton connects this early two-color tile workshop to the Chertsey tile workshop, which he suggests was working "at the same time or just a few years later." Norton also connects the use of inscriptions in the circular pavement for the king's chapel at Clarendon (c. 1240–1244), and in the Westminster chapter house (early–mid 1250s), to the inscriptions incorporated in the combat and Tristan series Chertsey tiles. For Norton, the use of complex inscriptions alongside or with all

[169] Lethaby, "Romance Tiles," 78.
[170] See Eames, *Catalogue*, 1: 165; Eames, *English Medieval Tiles*, 41; Alexander et al., *Age of Chivalry*, cat. no. 16.
[171] Eames, *English Medieval Tiles*, 41–43.
[172] Carpenter, "King Henry III and the Chapter House," 36.
[173] Noppen, *The Chapter House, Westminster Abbey*, 3.
[174] Norton, "The Luxury Pavement," 20.   [175] Ibid.

three of these inlaid-tile commissions is another feature that connects them.[176] Two of these three (the Clarendon circular pavement and Westminster chapter house) are known to be Henry III's commissions, and this provides yet another reason to believe that the Chertsey tiles were similarly royal commissions of roughly the same era.

The Antioch Chamber at Westminster Palace

Our digital reconstruction of the tiles' iconography and texts has revealed their strong connection to the Crusades. This recognition of the tiles' thematic focus, in conjunction with the general agreement on their likely commission by Henry III, encourages us to explore Henry and Eleanor's connections with the Crusades in the years around 1250, as well as any other artistic commissions the royal couple made in association with Crusading themes. On March 6, 1250, Henry III and Eleanor took the Cross, vowing to go on Crusade.[177] In 1252, Henry began formally collecting funds for his Crusade to the Holy Land, which he proclaimed would depart from England on June 24, 1256. Also in the mid-thirteenth century, a copy (known as Hatton 77) of a Crusading text, the *Siege d'Antioche*, was made probably for Henry's court.[178]

Additionally in 1250, a commission was recorded at Westminster Palace: the queen's chamber was to be decorated with the help of a book containing the "deeds of Antioch and of the king and others."[179] This room was later known as the Antioch chamber. This commission at Westminster was quickly followed by two additional Antioch chambers at the royal residences at Winchester and Clarendon commissioned in June and July of 1251 (Figure 39).[180] (An additional Antioch chamber was also commissioned for the Tower of London but never completed.)[181] The subject matter of "Antioch" should be understood not only as addressing the formerly Roman city on the Turkish/Syrian coast. To medieval men and women, it would have signaled the "deeds of Antioch," that is, the stories of Crusade. In medieval historical and troubadour traditions, the subject matter of Antioch is closely associated with the victorious First Crusade, in which the Latin met with smashing success in the Holy Land, including a notable battle at Antioch at which the tide seemed to turn, before the Crusaders finally took Jerusalem.

---

[176] Lethaby, *Westminster Abbey Re-Examined*, 113; Norton, "The Luxury Pavement," 21.
[177] Meuwese, "Antioch." [178] Carol Sweetenham, pers. comm., July 2019.
[179] Borenius, "The Cycle of Images," 45; Meuwese, "Antioch," 351; Whatley, "Romance, Crusade," 180.
[180] Borenius, "The Cycle of Images," 45; Vorderstrasse, "Trade and Textiles from Medieval Antioch," 170; Whatley, "Romance, Crusade," 181.
[181] Whatley, "Romance, Crusade," 181.

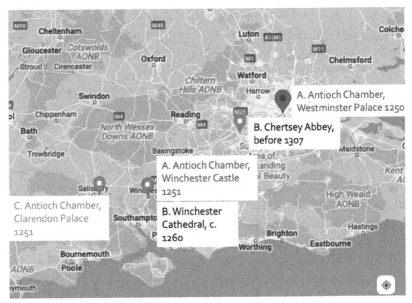

A = suggested site where Chertsey combat tiles were laid
B = documented findspot for Chertsey combat tiles
C = site where thematically connected tiles were found

Figure 39 Map showing documented and suggested sites in England where Chertsey combat tiles were laid. Created using Google Maps

It may well be coincidence that these unusual Crusades-themed floor tiles were apparently commissioned under English royal patronage in the years around 1250, and that four "Antioch" chambers, that is, chambers visually dedicated to Crusades material, were commissioned by the same patrons in the same time period. However, artwork made c. 1100–1300 specifically depicting the Crusades is rarer than one might imagine.[182] (Hence the role that the combat tiles' scene of Richard and Saladin has played in more recent exhibitions and educational frameworks.) Only one other example of Crusades-themed wall-painting connected to Henry III has been studied: this was a chapel showing biblical and Crusade stories connected to the True Cross, probably dating to Henry's boyhood, when his father, King John, vowed to go on Crusade.[183]

---

[182] Lapina et al., "Introduction," 6.
[183] Barrett, "Roland and Crusade Imagery," 129–168. In addition, a series of thirteenth-century Old Testament paintings at Westminster Palace can probably be understood in the light of the Crusades. The dating of these paintings has been debated. Binski, *The Painted Chamber at Westminster*, 22–24; Reeve, "The Painted Chamber at Westminster," 191; Wilson, "A Monument to St Edward," 161–169.

Due to the general rarity of Crusades-related art under Henry III, I am tempted to associate the commission of the Chertsey combat tiles with the commission of the Antioch chambers. Supporting evidence for a connection between the Antioch chambers and the combat tiles includes the description of the Antioch chamber at Clarendon Palace as containing both the story of Antioch and the duel of King Richard the Lionheart. That chamber's focus on Richard the Lionheart in a Crusading context precisely matches the combat tiles' focus. Initially, the medieval description of the third Antioch chamber as joining the story of Antioch and the duel of King Richard is confusing for a modern audience, as the story of Antioch specifically refers to the First Crusade, while Richard fought in the Third Crusade. While the deeds "of Antioch" were indeed most closely associated with the victorious First Crusade in the Middle Ages, that narrative lacks a notable English hero. While the Third Crusade ended with a truce, it has the virtue (for the English) of serving as a background for the bright narrative exploits of Richard, who was adopted by the English as the model of a Crusading king. The Clarendon chamber's apparently heterogeneous mixing of material from the traditions of the First ("Antioch") and the Third Crusades ("Richard the Lionheart") was unlikely to have bothered medieval individuals: the Crusades were only "numbered" after the Middle Ages.[184] What was more important to medieval audiences was the crafting of a particular kind of hero in a particular narrative context: an English Crusading king. This kind of hero would have salience during a period when the current English king was preparing to go on Crusade.

The Antioch chamber at Clarendon seems to have contained the same kind of combination of First and Third Crusade material that was exhibited in the Chertsey combat tiles. This kind of overlap was fairly common in written work, too, and presumably in the minds of educated observers. For instance, Carol Sweetenham describes the late twelfth-century Bishop of Canterbury, Baldwin, who was asked by his clerics for a recommendation for someone to write "the illustrious story of how the land of Palestine was won back by our nobles, of how Saladin and his Saracens were expelled by them."[185] As Sweetenham notes, "it is unclear how much this [request] refers to the First Crusade and how much to the Third."[186] Materials from "different" historical traditions were often conjoined to build medieval Crusading narratives in image and text.[187] In the case of the third Antioch chamber, a narrative of a victorious Richard was constructed against a background of other Crusading material. The same is true of the Chertsey combat tiles.

---

[184] Constable, *Crusaders and Crusading*, 353–356, Appendix B.
[185] Carol Sweetenham, pers. comm., July 2019.   [186] Ibid.   [187] Meuwese, "Antioch," 346.

The overlap in terms of specific subject matter, date, site, and royal patronage suggests the possibility that the combat tiles were commissioned in association with one of the Antioch chambers. If the combat tiles were initially intended for the first Antioch chamber (at Westminster Palace), their imagery could also have been complemented by wall painting, which Henry and Eleanor commissioned frequently. The decoration of this room at Westminster is known to have been informed by a manuscript, borrowed from the Templars' treasury, containing the "deeds of Antioch and of the king and others."[188] The tightly organized medallion pattern of the combat tiles would have provided a welcome formal complement to any painting on the wall. Indeed, the first Antioch chamber at Westminster seems to have impressed both its patron and audiences, for the commission was quickly repeated in other royal residences. What if its floor tiles – highly impressive, even for audiences today – were part of the reason for the success of the first Antioch chamber? This might help to explain the quick spread of Antioch chambers in other royal residences. Something about the room, certainly, was deemed highly successful and worthy of quickly duplicating elsewhere.

Even if the Chertsey combat tiles were not commissioned in conjunction with the Antioch chambers, their presence adjacent to any of these chambers would heighten a focus on Crusade. And in reverse, the import of the combat tiles would also be highlighted when viewed in the same vicinity as the Antioch chambers. Viewers would be primed, so to speak, to think Crusading thoughts. In addition, the image of Richard, an English Crusading king, presented anywhere in a royal palace would have been read in juxtaposition to the current English king, Henry III. The combat tiles, if they were laid in any royal palaces, would have served as positive publicity constructing Henry as the heir of the Crusading king Richard. Such an heir was desperately needed after the capture in February 1250 of the French king Louis IX in the Seventh Crusade.

The commission of the combat tile molds for the initial Westminster Antioch chamber is plausible but impossible to substantiate definitely. In this connection, however, it is telling that there are either physical or iconographical connections between the combat series tiles and each of the three sites of the Antioch chambers: Westminster, Winchester, and Clarendon – all, like Chertsey, in the southwest of England (Figure 39). The earliest commissioned Antioch chamber was the queen's chamber at Westminster. As already stated, previous research has connected the high-quality, secular subject, and drawing style of the Chertsey tiles to a set of secular square tiles laid in the chapter house

---

[188] Whatley, "Romance, Crusade," 180.

at Westminster Abbey. The second Antioch chamber was at the royal residence at Winchester. The only other spot where the combat tiles have been found, in addition to Chertsey abbey, is at Winchester Cathedral. Wessex tile designs used at Winchester Cathedral were also found at Winchester Castle. The discovery of the combat tiles at Winchester Cathedral could suggest their use in the nearby Antioch chamber at Winchester Castle. Finally, two tiles based on the combat tiles' iconography of the duel of Richard and Saladin were found at the third site, Clarendon.

It is plausible that the combat series Chertsey tiles were commissioned for the queen's Antioch chamber at Westminster, where artists and tile-makers were designing and firing secular narrative tiles that resemble those of the combat series. The final effect of the Antioch chamber at Westminster commissioned in 1250 was apparently deemed successful, judging by the two further commissions immediately following in June and July of 1251. Some of the Queen's chambers were damaged in a fire in 1298, the first of many instances of loss for the medieval palace of Westminster, including fires in 1512 and 1834, and so it is not surprising that no remnants of the Westminster Antioch chamber remain.[189] If the combat series tiles were indeed first used in the Antioch chamber at Westminster, it would make sense for the molds to be brought up to the second Antioch chamber at Winchester, so that more tiles could be fired and installed at Winchester Castle. This would explain the presence of combat series tiles in the nearby cathedral at Winchester. When work began at Clarendon during the summer of 1251, the combat tile molds might still have been in use at Winchester. Another set of combat tiles, loosely based on the iconography of the duel of Richard and Saladin, was then created and used instead at Clarendon. The original combat series molds were then brought to Chertsey and used there sometime before c. 1300. Such a series of events provides a reasonable rationale for the archeological finds as currently known, including the connection to Westminster, the presence of actual tiles at Winchester and Chertsey, and the iconographical connection to tiles at Clarendon.

If the combat tiles were commissioned in association with the first Antioch chamber, it follows that it was not necessarily Henry III who was initially responsible for these most impressive of English medieval tiles but rather Queen Eleanor of Provence. Certainly, the first Antioch chamber was commissioned not for the king's chambers but for the queen's. Margaret Howell has noted Queen Eleanor's personal engagement both in patronage and in Crusading affairs.[190] In 1250, Eleanor's sister, Margaret of Provence, had

---

[189] Crook, "Introduction to the Topography," 9.   [190] Howell, *Eleanor of Provence.*

traveled with her husband, King Louis IX of France, to the Holy Land as part of the Seventh Crusade, and it is highly likely that the sisters exchanged letters during this period.[191] Eleanor was an accomplished patron in her own right and not only in architectural spaces; she also purchased and owned manuscripts.[192] Indeed, some scholars have connected the striking and growing importance of floor tiles in royal palaces under Henry III more generally to Eleanor's influence – floor tiles being a more regular feature of continental productions until she married Henry in 1236, perhaps bringing ideas of floor tiles with her.[193] Female patronage in the Middle Ages is often disguised and unrecognized because of institutional tendencies (in both medieval and modern day) to keep records and organize information under the names of kings. Therefore, while it is far from certain that Eleanor was the original patron of the combat tiles, it is important to raise this possibility.

In this connection, one candidate for the author of Chertsey tile texts is a Latin poet whom Eleanor knew: John of Howden (fl. 1260s–1270s), who for a time served as clerk to Eleanor. He wrote verse both in Latin and in Anglo-Norman, including an Anglo-Norman poem, *Rossignos*, dedicated to Eleanor of Provence and which included Crusaders alongside other heroes.[194] Regardless of who composed the Chertsey tile texts – and we have no evidence as to their identity – it is helpful to imagine that their author could well have been someone like John of Howden: educated, fluent in Latin and Anglo-Norman, and in close contact with Eleanor. Creating juxtapositions between ancient and contemporary heroes is a theme that can be found not only in John of Howden's *Rossignos* but also in other coeval works. The theme of the Chertsey combat tiles, then, fits well with other cultural currents circulating around the royal court in the mid-thirteenth century.

5 Combats in Medallions: Cross-cultural Tiles and Textiles

This section presents an overview of the movement and imitation of medieval medallion silks, a global phenomenon. It then focuses on the presence of imported medallion silks in England and the connections between these treasured silks and the Chertsey combat pavement. Both the overall medallion composition of the Chertsey combat pavement (roundels set into a foliate surround, with smaller motifs in between) and the type of iconographic motifs (mounted archers, lion combats, and Samson) correspond precisely to specific genres of Islamic and Byzantine silks. These medallion combat silks and their

---

[191] Ibid., 60.   [192] Whatley, "Romance, Crusade," 183.
[193] James, *The Palaces of Medieval England*.
[194] Howell, *Eleanor of Provence*, 60, 83, 85, 93, 97–98, 248.

motifs, including the Parthian shot, were not valued only in the lands of their creation but across the medieval world. England was no exception.

The visual connection between the Chertsey combat pavement and imported medallion silks only became visible after we completed our digital reconstruction of the combat tile pavement (Figure 3). Before this digital reconstruction existed, the broken tile pieces were so small that it was difficult to grasp their original impact. Previous scholars focused, understandably, on recreating the iconography of each roundel. These drawings of individual roundels compared well with English and Western European pictorial iconographic sources like manuscripts. However, the combat mosaic was actually a large decorative surface marked by a pattern of regularly arranged roundels – a "medallion" pattern. The individual iconography of each roundel is of course significant, but it is experienced as part of a larger pattern. Our reconstruction of the pavement allows us to see that the English artists were impacted not just by Western European pictorial sources but also by another group of sources: imported medallion silks. Our reconstruction thereby enables us to reveal another genre of source material – a global genre – that previous scholars had not recognized.

As our digital reconstruction makes clear, the composition of the Chertsey combat floor set figural medallions into a foliate surround, with small motifs introduced at geometrically regular locations between the large medallions. Medallion pattern was common in ancient Rome in floor mosaic, among other forms. Beginning in the sixth century, medallion-patterned Byzantine textiles exploded in popularity and carried the compositional form both west and east, all the way to China, Korea, and Japan.[195] The popularity of medallion pattern was not limited to textiles, although textiles were its primary, highly prestigious carriers. A Korean pearl roundel relief sculpture, a Himalayan wall painting, and Germanic (Ottonian) manuscript all witness the appeal of figural medallion designs in the centuries around 1000 CE.[196] Still, while many patterns (including medallion pattern) travel between media, the preeminent and most prestigious carriers of medallion patterns were textiles, as established by James Trilling, Eva Hoffman, Lisa Golombek, Mary Margaret Fulghum, and others.[197]

Textiles were omnipresent in the medieval world. While this phenomenon has long been recognized in Asian and Islamic contexts, scholars have gradually

---

[195] Meister, "The Pearl Roundel in Chinese Textile Design"; Trilling, *The Medallion Style*; Trilling, "Medieval Interlace"; Trilling, *Ornament: A Modern Perspective*; Folda, "The Use of Cintamani"; Kim, "An Analysis of the Early Unified Silla."

[196] Kim, "An Analysis of the Early Unified Silla"; Flood, "Mobility and Mutation"; Fidler and Levy, "The Date of the Alchi Sumtsek Murals"; Garrison, "Mimetic Bodies."

[197] Trilling, *The Medallion Style*; Golombek, "The Draped Universe of Islam"; Trilling, "Medieval Interlace"; Hoffman, "Pathways of Portability"; Fulghum, "Under Wraps"; Trilling, *Ornament: A Modern Perspective*; Bier, "Pattern Power."

begun to see its truth across cultures, including those of Western Europe.[198] Textiles were carried vast distances because of their value within medieval societies. They were among the most expensive objects a medieval individual or institution might own, partly because they could be woven with gold and set with precious gemstones.[199] Colors made from exclusive pigments, complexity of pattern, rarity, and indeed the material of silk could all hold social and financial value. As a form of mobile and easily displayed wealth, textiles accompanied the lay and religious global elite on their travels, where they acted as important mobile markers of status, as they could be spread across walls and furniture to transform temporary chambers into elite spaces. Transported textiles could also be worn during meetings, feasts, or attendance at religious ceremonies. Imported medallion silks, like all imported silks, were expensive and highly valued as gifts and on the open market.

Finally, however, a medallion composition is only one of three connections with imported silks made manifest by the Chertsey tiles. In brief, the combat tiles share their medallion composition, combat iconography, and presence in elite interiors with imported silks, and it is this combination of factors which supports viewing the combat tiles in dialogue with textiles. It is possible that the appearance of these combat-themed medallion silks inspired the combat tiles' designers; it is also possible that medieval viewers would have connected the appearance of the floor to imported medallion textiles bearing combat themes. Side-by-side comparisons between combat silks – worn or hung – in the same spaces as the combat tiles would enable another level of understanding. Subtle adaptation in the iconography of the combat tiles when compared to the silks – on the tiles, English fighters now take the place of the combatants of foreign appearance, as found on imported silks – was one of the more powerful features of the pavement.

The movement of motifs back and forth from tile to textile can be followed not just through centuries but through millennia and across many geographical regions. Both tiles and textiles are intended to cover large interior surfaces. In addition, by the mechanical nature of their production (through molds or looms), both tiles and textiles display repeated images through which they

---

[198] Baker, *Islamic Textiles*; Watt, Wardwell, and Rossabi, *When Silk Was Gold: Central Asian and Chinese Textiles*; Gordon, *Robes and Honor: The Medieval World of Investiture*; Allsen, "Robing in the Mongolian Empire"; Fleming, "Acquiring, Flaunting and Destroying"; Canepa, "Textiles and Elite Tastes"; Desrosiers, "Chinese Silks in the Merovingian Graves of Saint-Denis Basilica?"; Fircks and Schorta, *Oriental Silks in Medieval Europe*; Hildebrandt and Gillis, *Silk: Trade and Exchange*; Blessing, "The Textile Museum Journal – Draping the Middle Ages"; Williams, "A Taste for Textiles: Designing Umayyad and 'Abbāsid Interiors'"; Blessing et al., *Medieval Textiles across Eurasia*.

[199] Smith, Fleming, and Halpin, "Court and Piety in Late Anglo-Saxon England," 586.

cover large interior surfaces. These practical similarities exist alongside their semiconstant elbow-jostling in public and private spaces for millennia. Examples of specific patterns crossing between textiles and tiles are many. As Trilling noted, it was common for designs to transfer from mosaic to textile in late antiquity.[200] Across the fifth century in the Mediterranean, Gonosová traces the use of particular patterns (the structured floral semis and diagonal diaper) in mosaics and other media and concludes that the use of these patterns in non-textile media "coincided with a more frequent use of the patterned silks themselves."[201] In early Islamic palaces like Khirbat al-Mafjar outside Jericho, the patterns found in stucco panels on walls imitated textiles.[202] Later Islamic cultures, like the Nasrids in Spain and the Ottomans in Turkey, also show design crossover between textiles (like curtains) and tiled wall decor, or ceiling decor, or tiled floors. Nor was the crossover between floor and textile patterns foreign to England – Lindy Grant has suggested that the Westminster cosmati pavement was inspired by Henry III's coronation cloak.[203]

Silks with Combat Scenes, Recorded in English Inventories

Imported medallion textiles bearing combat scenes were gifted and displayed in thirteenth-century England, as is witnessed in English inventories.[204] The royal family and other English elites owned silks depicting mounted archers, lion combats, and Samson, which they then later donated to St. Paul's, and we can imagine such textiles worn and displayed at public and ceremonial events. For instance, the 1295 St. Paul's inventory shows that Henry III owned multiple imported silk textiles, often referred to as "baudekins," including one depicting Samson "the strong": "A purple baudekin with columns and arcades, and Samson the Strong under the arcade, by gift of King Henry."[205] Samson "the strong" also appears in the Chertsey combat medallions, where we see the scene of Samson breaking the lion's mouth. It is possible that Henry's textile showed Samson engaged in this same action. Another textile also at St. Paul's certainly showed this very scene on a red baudekin: "A red baudekin, with Samson binding the lion's mouth, given by Almaric de Lucy, for the soul of G. de Lucy."[206]

The 1295 inventory also records that Henry III's son, Edward I, and his wife, Eleanor of Castile, gifted to St. Paul's a red baudekin ornamented with mounted

---

[200] Trilling, *The Medallion Style.*   [201] Gonosová, "The Formation and Sources," 237.
[202] Taragan, "Textiles in Cross-cultural Encounters."   [203] Grant, "The Coronation Mantle."
[204] For full documentation, see my forthcoming book, tentatively titled *English Bodies, Imported Silks.*
[205] Dugdale and Ellis, *The History of Saint Paul's*, 328. Translation by the author.
[206] Ibid. Translation by the author.

knights in roundels: "Two red baudekins, with archers inside the wheels, from the gift of Edward the King, and the Queen, coming from Wales."[207] Indeed, at St. Paul's in 1295 were also two additional silks with images of mounted knights in a medallion pattern; one of these had been gifted by King Edward I, and the other by the bishop of London Henry of Sandwich (D. 1273). These are described as follows: "A purple baudekin, with knights riding horseback, and birds inside the wheels, from a gift of Edward the King;" "Cope given by Henry of Sandwich, Bishop of London, made of baudekin 'in the manner of temples' with knights riding inside [the wheels], with birds on their hands."[208] At St. Paul's in 1295, there were, then, at least three silks with images of mounted knights in roundels, and in all three cases these were gifted by significant historical figures who, quite probably, had displayed these textiles for their own uses before gifting them to St. Paul's. All three of these would have borne visual similarities to the Chertsey combat pavement.

In addition, twenty-three other silks recorded at St. Paul's in 1245 or 1295, at Exeter cathedral, or in medieval English private collections also displayed combat iconography which compares well to that of the combat mosaic.[209] These silks are not explicitly named as medallion silks, but they may well have been such. Silk iconography is recorded inconsistently in medieval inventories, and extant medieval silks with combat iconography frequently (although certainly not always) bear medallion patterns. The relevant recorded silks are named, for instance, as "baudekin with knights riding horses," or "cope made from baudekin with men riding horses." Other examples include "baudekin with armed knights," "baudekin with crossbowmen," "cloth with lions and archers," "baudekin with archers," "cope with archers," "cloth with kings riding horseback in circles between arctuated columns." These subjects are close to those of the combat tiles, which also included images of knights riding horses, armed knights, archers, crossbowmen, and kings riding horseback.

Extant Silks with Combat Scenes

Sadly, none of these recorded textiles from St. Paul's, Exeter, or English private collections survive today. However, it is not difficult to find surviving silks that correspond to these descriptions of combat scenes, often inside medallions, including lion combats on foot, mounted archers fighting lions, and mounted

---

[207] Ibid. Translation by the author. For more information on this record, see Luyster, "Reassembling Textile Networks."

[208] Dugdale et al., *The History of Saint Paul's*, 328. Translation by the author.

[209] All listed in Lehmann-Brockhaus, *Lateinische Schriftquellen*. For full documentation, see my forthcoming book, tentatively titled *English Bodies, Imported Silks*.

soldiers – sometimes mounted rulers – wielding lances against lions.[210] These silks have been attributed to al-Andalus (Islamic Spain), the eastern Mediterranean, Central Asia, and beyond. For instance, lion fights on foot appear on a sixth- or seventh-century Syrian silk (Figure 40) showing an archer aiming his bow at a lion. Mounted archers and lions can be found on another silk attributed to seventh-century Syria (Figure 41). This silk also includes the Parthian shot. Mounted archers are also included in the hunter and

Figure 40 Textile fragment showing huntsman and lion, sixth or seventh century. Silk twill. The Keir Collection of Islamic Art on loan to the Dallas Museum of Art, K.1.2014.1220. © The Dallas Museum of Art

---

[210] Muthesius, *Byzantine Silk Weaving*; Brubaker and Haldon, *Byzantium: The Sources*, 93; Schrenk, *Textilien des Mittelmeerraumes*, 293–294, 318–319; Brubaker and Haldon, *Byzantium: A History*, 336–347; Walker, *The Emperor and the World*, 28–29; Mackie, *Symbols of Power*, 49–50 and passim.

Figure 41 Medallion silk with horseman aiming a bow at a lion. Seventh century, probably Syrian. Church treasury of St. Servatius, Maastricht. Inv. No. SSS1113. © Schatkamer Sint Servaas Maastricht

Amazon silks. Some of the hunter and Amazon silks have been ascribed to eighth-century Byzantine origins, while others are probably Islamic. Finally, mounted soldiers using lances against lions ornament an eighth- or ninth-century Byzantine silk conserved at Lyon (Figure 42) and a ninth-century samite attributed to eastern Iran or Central Asia (Figure 43).

While many of these silks bear images of hunters and soldiers in roundels, in most cases, the main motifs are doubled in a single medallion. The doubling and sometimes quadrupling of a figural motif, as if reflected across a horizontal or vertical axis, can be programmed into loom threads.[211] This doubling across an axis, so characteristic of many silks, is not reproduced in the combat tiles. The

---

[211] Blessing et al., *Medieval Textiles Across Eurasia.*

Figure 42 Silk showing mounted emperors (?) and lions, known as the "Shroud of St. Austremoine" or the "Shroud of Mozac." Byzantine, probably Constantinople, eighth or first half of the ninth century. Lyon, Musée des Tissus MT 27386. Acquired from the church of Mozac, 1904. © Lyon, Musée des Tissus – Pierre Verrier

Figure 43 Samite roundels with hunters. Eastern Iran or Central Asia, ninth century. Cleveland Museum of Art, Purchase from the J. H. Wade Fund, 1982.284

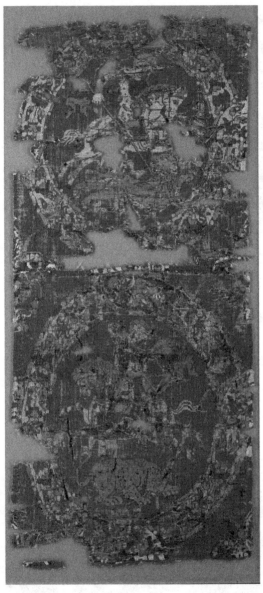

Figure 44 Rider with a lance spearing a lion. Sixth- to ninth-century, Byzantine. Victoria & Albert Museum, 559–1893. © Victoria and Albert Museum, London

combat tiles, made from molds, use a different kind of technology to create a repeat. Each tile mold carries a single motif, but the same mold could be used to create a large number of separate tile roundels. However, single (not doubled) motifs, as on the Chertsey tiles, can be found on some silks. For instance, a sixth- to ninth-century Byzantine (Coptic?) textile in the Victoria & Albert

Museum shows mounted soldiers with arrows and mounted horsemen with lances, both attacking lions, not doubled, in roundels (Figure 44). A fragment from Dumbarton Oaks has been associated with the Victoria & Albert piece.[212] Both fragments of this textile have been associated with the better-known Annunciation and Nativity silks from the Cappella Sancta Sanctorum in Rome, which have been attributed to Byzantine or Coptic manufacture.[213] Both the fragments at the Victoria & Albert Museum and Dumbarton Oaks and the combat tiles, then, show scenes of mounted combats, often with lions, with the single (not doubled) motifs showing small variations from each other, in thickly framed roundels, alternating with foliate patterns. The textile fragments of course originally would have been part of panels of whole cloth, extending in a grid of roundels like the tiles. These fragments from the Victoria & Albert Museum and Dumbarton Oaks show a strong resemblance both in composition and iconography to the Chertsey combat tiles.

Similarly, the Bishop Gurb silk (Figure 45), probably made in Spain in the early thirteenth century (just a few decades before the Chertsey tiles), includes some court scenes and horsemen in roundels, surrounded by text or pseudo-text, without the doubling of the main motif and with variations in the forms of the horsemen. Both this textile and the Chertsey tiles, then, show scenes of mounted horsemen with the single (not doubled) motifs showing small variations from each other,

Figure 45 Celestial banquet hanging (fragment), from the tomb of Bishop Gurb (d. 1284). Spain, probably Almeria, thirteenth century. Cleveland Museum of Art, purchase from the J. H. Wade Fund, 1966.368

---

[212] The fragment at Dumbarton Oaks is BZ.1937.29.

[213] The Annunciation silk, as Figure 21, is discussed in Blessing et al., *Medieval Textiles Across Eurasia*. The two bands and intervening ornament on the mounted soldier textile are identical with those on silk representing the Annunciation and Nativity. The fragments are 558–1893 and 561–1893 at the Victoria & Albert Museum.

in thickly framed roundels including text. The Bishop Gurb textile is joined by a small group of probably Spanish textiles, including the so-called Chasuble of Thomas Becket in Fermo, which may be fruitfully examined alongside the Chertsey tiles.[214] All of these textiles – the hunter, Amazon, and single-motif horseman silks – provide a significant vantage point from which to understand the Chertsey tiles and their focus on mounted horsemen, rulers, archers, and lions in medallions.

Acquisition of Silk on Crusade

While silk had been present in significant ways in England since Anglo-Saxon times, the advent of the Crusades in 1095 – and specifically the fall of silk-rich Constantinople during the Fourth Crusade in 1204 – increased the number and arguably the significance of imported silks in thirteenth-century England.[215] First of all, *more* silks arrived in England after the beginning of the Crusades. Crusaders brought home easily packable silks along with relics and other mementoes from their time abroad. In addition, the Crusades accompanied (and probably promoted) increased exchange between the Latin West and the Mediterranean east; so more silks were circulating through Western Europe through trade, too.[216] Indeed, in the thirteenth century, trade in silks in England was substantial. For example, Henry III purchased a number of silks from Adam de Basing, who was both a merchant and ran a textile workshop in which imported silks could be tailored.[217]

And finally, the stories told in England about silks in the Crusades era were no longer just narratives of imperial authority and sacred history; they now included military exploits. Many Crusaders – who were often also pilgrims but whose military service was an important part of their experience in the Holy Land – returned home with textiles. Individuals, families, and institutions created material histories based on objects that came home from the Crusades.[218] Textiles brought home from the Crusades could then be offered, gifted, and displayed in the context of stories not just about empire and holiness but also vivid first-person recollections of battle. Imported silks in England would thereby often be presented and collected in the narrative context of valiant deeds accomplished overseas. The combat tiles, similar in appearance, are also similar in function.

---

[214] Shalem, *The Chasuble of Thomas Becket*.
[215] Dodwell, *Anglo-Saxon Art: A New Perspective*, 129–169; Fleming, "Acquiring, Flaunting and Destroying," 132; Owen-Crocker and Coatsworth, *Encyclopaedia*, s.v. "Silk: Silk Road."
[216] Jacoby, "Silk Crosses the Mediterranean"; Jacoby, "Silk Economics."
[217] Lancaster, "Artists, Suppliers and Clerks," esp. 87–89.
[218] Klein, "Eastern Objects and Western Desires"; Paul, *To Follow in Their Footsteps*; Lester, "Intimacy and Abundance."

Conclusion: Carpets, Clay, and Foreigners

When the combat tiles were laid in a panel as part of a floor, advancing across its surface would have suggested walking across panels of imported textiles. Fine textiles on the floor have an ancient history of two intertwined associations: they may suggest near-divine honor and, at the same time, potential hubris due to their very excess. In the ancient Greek play *Agamemnon* (lines 905–974) by Aeschylus, Clytemnestra invites her husband, Agamemnon, who has just returned from conquering Troy, to enter his palace by walking upon an incredibly expensive purple-dyed textile.[219] Agamemnon hesitates to walk on the expensive cloth because "It is the gods who should be honored with such things," not mortal men. He also refuses to do so because it is too feminine: the long-lived trope of a feminized east, still part of medieval Crusading texts, is present here.[220] Finally, he associates walking on purple cloth with the fawning treatment offered to oriental monarchs (at least in Greek sources): "do not, in the manner of a barbarian man, fall to the ground before me and utter a cry with a gaping mouth."

While most medieval English observers were unlikely to have been aware of this passage from Aeschylus, these dueling interpretations of carpet – as well-deserved and near-divine honor, or as inappropriate, foreign, and potentially feminizing excess – could well have remained at play in thirteenth-century England. In 1255, the brother of the king of Castile, Sancho, who was also the bishop-elect of Toledo, arrived in London. The English historian Matthew Paris remarks upon Sancho's youth – he was only twenty years old – and also how he "ornamented his place of abode, which was at the New Temple, and even the floor of it, with tapestries, palls, and curtains."[221] Clearly some of the English were impressed with Sancho's home décor, as word of it reached Matthew Paris, although it is not clear that such luxury met with broad approval, as Paris continues on to mention that the citizens of London taunted Sancho and his attendants with "gluttony and luxuriousness." Similarly, when Eleanor of Castile, Sancho's sister and Edward I's new wife, entered London for the first time in October 1255, Matthew Paris describes a similar phenomenon.

> When the noble princess arrived at the lodging assigned to her, she found it, like the hotel of the bishop-elect of Toledo, hung with rich silk cloths and tapestries, looking like a church, and even the floors were covered in this

---

[219] I am grateful to Mary Ebbott for bringing this passage to my attention.

[220] Akbari, *Idols in the East*.

[221] I am grateful to Tom Nickson for this reference. Giles and Rishanger, *Matthew Paris's English History*, vol. 3, 132.

manner. This was done by the Spanish, it being the custom in their country, but their excessive pride in this moved the people to both laughter and derision. Serious and wise people, weighing up events to come, were deeply grieved after careful consideration of the pleasure shown by the king at the presence of the foreigners .... The English therefore regretted that they themselves were held in less esteem by the king than the people of other nations, and sorrowfully realized that their irreparable ruin was imminent.[222]

In this instance, it seems likely that the silks used had been brought from Spain, as the decoration of the rooms "was done by the Spanish," and again, the precious cloths were, to the amazement (and derision) of the English, spread on the floor. As Thomas Tolley notes, this passage also suggests that there was a "special Spanish way of doing things with reference to the visual arts"; that this was "alien to England"; and that the king's approving response to this Castilian display was read politically; that is, that the king favored "aliens" over the native-born English.[223] Intriguingly, this historical record suggests that the use of specific textile traditions, particularly those not native to England, can be read as political acts with moral overtones (English witnesses disapprove with emotion: derision, laughter, and anger). Elaborately patterned tiles made to look like textiles, however, would appeal to both cosmopolitan and local audiences, as the textile-patterned tiles allude to foreign traditions and luxury, while being English-made and avoiding material excess. It is not an act of hubris to walk across ceramic tiles, nor are ceramic tiles alien – at least by the mid-thirteenth-century – to English floors.

The Chertsey combat pavement could visually allude to the rich silk traditions of other lands, yet its medium eschewed the luxury of silk for the homegrown appeal of humble English clay. It was, perhaps, a perfect pavement for wealthy English patrons in the 1250s: the Chertsey combat floor reflects their fascination with the lands and cultural productions of faraway worlds, while affirming both in its iconography and its materiality the ultimate dominance of the English. Our study of the glocal phenomenon of the Chertsey tiles then reveals the pull of both poles: the attraction of the global, alongside an insistence on the priority of the local.

---

[222] Luard, *Matthaei Parisiensis*, v. 513; Tolley, "Eleanor of Castile and the 'Spanish' Style," 178.
[223] Tolley, "Eleanor of Castile and the 'Spanish' Style," 178–179.

Appendix

Eighty-five text fragments remain to us. I have published elsewhere our method in reassembling the textual fragments into words and sometimes phrases.[224] This method required an examination of the textual fragments extant on Chertsey tiles, vocabulary used in Crusading narratives, and two Latin frequency dictionaries. Possible words were generated from the text fragment, which were matched both against Crusading texts and frequency dictionaries. We also took into account, when relevant, the less-well-known "second series" of Chertsey texts. Molds for the Chertsey combat series roundels remained in use for some years (decades, probably) after their first use.[225] In later years, they were laid not in the complex mosaic of their original design but in a simpler arrangement. This later, less complicated arrangement reused at least some of the same texts that were found on the earlier small mosaic tiles. In some cases, the later frame tiles provide longer texts than were found in the originals. For instance, LEO survives from the Chertsey combat first series texts; while A: LEONIS : survives in the second series texts (Figure 32).[226] To my knowledge, no sustained study has ever been made of the second series texts.

While I have a firm rationale for the reconstructive decisions I have made, the final interpretation of each fragment is just that: an interpretation. While we might wish that human judgment had no place in this reconstruction, in reality this is a complex process with a number of variables. I submit these interpretations in all humility, and I welcome later attempts and improvements on this initial endeavor. I offer these results as a robust first attempt at finding meaning in these heretofore unexamined inscriptional fragments.

---

[224] Luyster, "Fragmented Tile, Fragmented Text."
[225] Eames, *Catalogue*, 1: 141–171 and esp. 165.
[226] British Museum 1885,1113.10654; Chertsey Museum CHYMS.2000.008.

Table A1 Fragments and "most likely" words

Eames design no.	Characters present	With abbreviations expanded	Most likely word	Meaning
688	:GLI	:GLI	:GLI/SCO	I grow in power/violence
674	:RICA	:RICA	:RICA/RDO	By (or to/for) Richard
750	:Ro	:Ro	Ricardo	By (or to/for) Richard
685	~SAM	Samson	SAMson	Samson
667	ACCI	ACCI	ACCI/DIT	Happens
689	AVD	AUD	AUD/ET: (or possibly AUD/AX)	He dares or the bold/rash one
690	BAC	BAC	BAC/ULO	By the stick (or, less likely: to/for the stick)
691	BEL	BEL	BEL/LA or BEL/LA:VI	Wars or combats (or possibly but unlikely "You fight!")
718	C#Ri	C'RERI or C'RARI	CONTRARII	Enemies, of the enemy, or hostile
668	FIGI	FIGI	FIGI/T' (TUR), FIGI, FIGI/t, : or possibly :E/FIGI/ET	He pierces/transfixes [with a weapon], or he is pierced/transfixed, or let him portray
699	FRE	FRE	FRE/GI: or FRE/TI or FRE/TUS	I broke/subdued OR relying on, supported by
678	GAT	GRAT	GRAT/IA:	Grace, or by grace

700	GLI	GLI	AN/GLI or AN/GLI/e seems most likely. Possibly FOR/TIUS:EN/GLI but this spelling is unexpected Another, less likely, option is NE/GLI/GI	Of England, of the Englishman, the English, or to be ignored
719	GVe:	GUE:	UN/GUE:	By claw/talon
702	hAS	hAS	HAS/TA: or, less likely, HAS (here or these)	The spear/by the spear or HAS (these)
703	hIC	hIC	hIC	Here or this
704	hIC	hIC	hIC	Here or this
705	LEO	LEO	LEO and also LEONIS.	Lion (and/or of the lion)
679	MAG	MAGN, MANG, MAGAN, MAGAM	Some form of MAGN/us MAGN/a MAGN/um (could be MAGN/O:?)	Great/ by (or to/for) a great
680	MORS	MORS	MORS	Death
670	NERE	NERARE or NERAVERE	VUL/NERARE or VUL/NERAVERE	To wound, you are wounded, they wounded
681	O:MI	O:MI	O:MI/LES or O:MI/li/TIS (second series)	The knight/of the knight
709	ORA	ORA	ORA	Jaws
671	ORIA:	ORIA:	gl/ORIA or vict/ORIA	Glory or by glory, victory or by victory
672	PERIT	PERIT	PERIT	He perishes
673	QUID	QUID	QUID	Something/anything; [the thing] that/which

Table A1 (cont.)

Eames design no.	Characters present	With abbreviations expanded	Most likely word	Meaning
682	QVI:	QUI:	QUI:	Who/that
711	REX	REX	REX	King (the king)
722	RT	RTUS	LA:VI/RTUS	Courage, strength, or army
684	RvIS	RUIS	RUIS or NE/RUIS	You ruin/destroy/charge; by or to/for bows/muscles/nerves
712	SEL	SEL	SEL/LIA/DEN	Saladin
713	TEG	TEG	TEG/O:	I cover/protect/defend
675	TI:EN (object page says M:EN)	TIUS:EN	FOR/TIUS:EN, possibly FOR/TIUS:EN/sis or FOR/TIUS:EN/GLI	Quite strong/brave or quite bravely . . . (possibly, more bravely the sword or more bravely the English)
676	VIRT	VIRTUS	VIRTUS (VIRTUS : S is from design 871)	Courage, strength, or army

Bibliography

Akbari, Suzanne Conklin. *Idols in the East: European Representations of Islam and the Orient, 1100–1450*. Ithaca: Cornell University Press, 2009.

Albin, Andrew, Mary Carpenter Erler, Thomas O'Donnell, Nicholas Paul, and Nina Rowe, eds. *Whose Middle Ages? Teachable Moments for an Ill-Used Past*. New York: Fordham University Press, 2019.

Alexander, Jonathan James Graham, and Paul Binski. *Age of Chivalry: Art in Plantagenet England, 1200–1400*. London: Royal Academy of Arts, 1987.

Allsen, Thomas T. "Robing in the Mongolian Empire." In *Robes and Honor: The Medieval World of Investiture*, edited by Stewart Gordon, 305–313. New York: Palgrave, 2001.

The Royal Hunt in Eurasian History. Philadelphia: University of Pennsylvania Press, 2011.

Ambrose, Kirk. "Samson, David, or Hercules? Ambiguous Identities in Some Romanesque Sculptures of Lion Fighters." *Konsthistorisk Tidskrift* 74, no. 3 (2005): 1–17.

Anderlini, Tina. "Dressing the Sacred: Medallion Silks and Their Use in Western Medieval Europe." In *Medieval Clothing and Textiles 15*, edited by Monica L. Wright, Robin Netherton, and Gale R. Owen-Crocker, 101–136. Woodbridge : Boydell and Brewer, 2019.

Baker, Patricia L. *Islamic Textiles*. London: British Museum Press, 1995.

Barrett, Christopher. "Roland and Crusade Imagery in an English Royal Chapel: Early Thirteenth-Century Wall Paintings in Claverley Church, Shropshire." *The Antiquaries Journal* 92 (2012): 129–168.

Besson, François Marie. "'A armes égales': Une Représentation de la violence en France et en Espagne au XIIe siècle." *Gesta* 26 no. 2 (1987): 113–126.

Betts, Ian M. *Medieval "Westminster" Floor Tiles*. MoLAS Monograph. London: Museum of London, November 15, 2002.

Bier, Carol. "Pattern Power: Textiles and the Transmission of Knowledge." *Textile Society of America Symposium Proceedings* no. 444 (2004).

Binski, Paul. *The Painted Chamber at Westminster*. London: Society of Antiquaries of London, 1986.

Bishop, Adam. "Usama Ibn Munqidh and Crusader Law in the Twelfth Century." *Crusades* 12 (2013): 53–65.

Blessing, Patricia. "Draping, Wrapping, Hanging: Transposing Textile Materiality in the Middle Ages." *The Textile Museum Journal* 45, (2018): 2–21.

"The Textile Museum Journal – Draping the Middle Ages." 45 (2018).

Blessing, Patricia, Eiren L. Shea, and Elizabeth Dospĕl Williams. *Medieval Textiles Across Eurasia, c. 300–1500.* The Global Middle Ages. Cambridge: Cambridge University Press, 2023.

Borenius, Tancred. "The Cycle of Images in the Palaces and Castles of Henry III." *Journal of the Warburg and Courtauld Institutes* 6 (1943): 40–50.

Bostock, John, ed. *The Natural History of Pliny the Elder.* London: D. L. Bell, 1893.

Brereton, Gareth, ed. *I am Ashurbanipal King of the World, King of Assyria: The BP Exhibition.* London: Thames & Hudson/The British Museum, 2019.

Brubaker, Leslie and John F. Haldon. *Byzantium in the Iconoclast Era (c.680–850), the Sources: An Annotated Survey.* Aldershot: Ashgate, 2001.

Byzantium in the Iconoclast Era (c. 680–850): A History. Cambridge: Cambridge University Press, 2011.

Calkin, Siobhain Bly. *Saracens and the Making of English Identity: The Auchinleck Manuscript.* Abingdon: Routledge, 2013.

Camille, Michael. "Gothic Signs and the Surplus: The Kiss on the Cathedral." *Yale French Studies: Contexts: Style and Value in Medieval Literature* (1991): 151–170.

Canepa, Matthew P. "Textiles and Elite Tastes Between the Mediterranean, Iran and Asia at the End of Antiquity." In *Global Textile Encounters*, edited by Marie-Louise Nosch, Feng Zhao, and Lotika Varadarajan, 1–14. Philadelphia: Oxbow Books, 2015.

Carpenter, David A. "King Henry III and the Cosmati Work at Westminster Abbey." In John Blair and Brian Golding, eds. *Cloister and the World: Essays in Medieval History in Honour of Barbara Harvey*, 178–195. Oxford: Clarendon, 1996.

"King Henry III and the Chapter House of Westminster Abbey." In *Westminster Abbey Chapter House: The History, Art and Architecture of "a Chapter House Beyond Compare,"* edited by Warwick Rodwell and Richard Mortimer, 32–39. London: Society of Antiquaries of London, 2010.

Constable, Giles. *Crusaders and Crusading in the Twelfth Century.* Farnham: Ashgate, 2008.

Craib, Theodore. *The Itinerary of Henry III 1216–1272, Report Completed in the Public Record Office in 1923, Edited and Annotated with Introduction and Analysis by S Brindle & S Priestley.* 1923.

Crockford, Julie E. "The Itinerary of Edward I of England: Pleasure, Piety, and Governance." In Alison L. Gascoigne, Leonie V. Hicks, and Marianne O'Doherty, eds. *Journeying Along Medieval Routes in Europe and the Middle East*, 231–257. Turnhout: Brepols, 2016.

Crook, John. "An Introduction to the Topography of the Medieval Palace of Westminster." In *Westminster: II. The Art, Architecture and Archaeology of the Royal Palace*, edited by Warwick Rodwell and Tim Tatton-Brown, 1–21. Leeds : Maney Publishing for the British Archaeological Association Conference Transactions, 2015.

Dale, Thomas E. A. *Relics, Prayer, and Politics in Medieval Venetia: Romanesque Painting in the Crypt of Aquileia Cathedral*. Princeton: Princeton University Press, 1997.

Desrosiers, Sophie. "Chinese Silks in the Merovingian Graves of Saint-Denis Basilica?" In *Aspects of the Design, Production and Use of Textiles and Clothing from the Bronze Age to the Early Modern Era*, edited by Karina Grömer and Frances Pritchard, 135–143. Budapest: Archaeolingua, 2015.

Dinkova-Bruun, Greti. "Biblical Thematics: The Story of Samson in Medieval Literary Discourse." *Oxford Handbooks Online*. Oxford: Oxford University Press, (2012). https://doi.org/10.1093/OXFORDHB/97801953 94016.013.0017.

Dodwell, Charles R. *Anglo-Saxon Art: A New Perspective*. Ithaca: Cornell University Press, 1985.

Dugdale, William and Henry Ellis. *The History of Saint Paul's Cathedral, in London, from Its Foundation: Extracted out of Original Charters, Records, Leiger-Books, and Other Manuscripts*. London: Lackington, Hughes, Harding, Mavor, and Jones, 1818.

Eames, Elizabeth. "A Decorated Tile Pavement from the Queen's Chamber, Clarendon Palace, Wiltshire, Dated 1250–1252." *The British Museum Quarterly* 22, no. 1/2 (1960): 34–37.

Catalogue of Medieval Lead-Glazed Earthenware Tiles in the Department of Medieval and Later Antiquities, British Museum. Vols. 2. London: British Museum, 1980.

English Medieval Tiles. London: Trustees of the British Museum, 1985.

Eames, Elizabeth and J. S. Gardner. "A Tile Kiln at Chertsey Abbey." *Journal of the British Archaeological Association* XVII (1954): 24–50.

Ellard, Donna-Beth. *Anglo-Saxon(ist) Pasts, PostSaxon Futures*. Brooklyn: Punctum books, 2019.

Feltham, Heleanor B. "Lions, Silks and Silver: The Influence of Sasanian Persia." *Sino-Platonic Papers* 206 (2010):1–51.

Fergusson, Peter. "Canterbury Cathedral Priory's Bath House and Fish Pond." In *Anglo-Norman Studies XXXVII: Proceedings of the Battle Conference*, edited by Elisabeth van Houts, 115–130. Woodbridge: Boydell, 2014.

Fergusson, Peter and Stuart Harrison. *Rievaulx Abbey: Community, Architecture, Memory.* New Haven: Yale University Press, 1999.

Fidler, Luke and Rachel Q. Levy. "The Date of the Alchi Sumtsek Murals: 11th or 13th Century?" *Ladakh Studies* 31 (2014): 37–38.

Fircks, Juliane von and Regula Schorta. *Oriental Silks in Medieval Europe.* Riggisberg: Abegg-Stiftung, 2016.

Fleming, Robin. "Acquiring, Flaunting and Destroying Silk in Late Anglo-Saxon England." *Early Medieval Europe* 15 (2007): 127–158.

Flood, Finbarr Barry. "Mobility and Mutation: Iranian Hunting Themes in the Murals of Alchi, Western Himalayas." *South Asian Studies* 7, no. 1 (1991): 21–35.

Folda, Jaroslav. "The Use of Cintamani as Ornament: A Case Study in the Afterlife of Forms." In *Byzantine Images and Their Afterlives: Essays in Honor of Annemarie Weyl Carr*, edited by Lynn Jones. Burlington: Ashgate, 2014.

Forsyth, Ilene H. "The Samson Monolith." In Caroline Bruzelius and Jill Meredith, eds. *The Brummer Collection of Medieval Art*, 20–55. Durham: Duke University Press, 1991.

Fulghum, Mary Margaret. "Under Wraps: Byzantine Textiles as Major and Minor Arts." *Studies in the Decorative Arts* 9, no. 1 (2001): 13–33.

Furrow, Melissa M. *Expectations of Romance: The Reception of a Genre in Medieval England.* Cambridge: D. S. Brewer, 2009.

Garrison, Eliza. "Mimetic Bodies: Repetition, Replication, and Simulation in the Marriage Charter of Empress Theophanu." *Word & Image* 33, no. 2 (2017): 212–232.

Gasparini, Mariachiara. "Sino-Iranian Textile Patterns in Trans-Himalayan Areas." *The Silk Road* 14 (2016): 84–96.

Transcending Patterns: Silk Road Cultural and Artistic Interactions through Central Asian Textile Images. Honolulu: University of Hawai'i Press, 2020.

Giles, John Allen and William Rishanger, eds. *Matthew Paris's English History. From the Year 1235 to 1273.* London: H. G. Bohn, 1852.

Gillingham, John B. "Some Legends of Richard the Lionheart: Their Development and Their Influence." In *Richard Coeur de Lion in History and Myth*, edited by Janet L. Nelson, 51–69. London: Centre for Late Antique and Medieval Studies, King's College, 1992.

Gilyard-Beer, R. "Byland Abbey and the Grave of Roger de Mowbray." *Yorkshire Archaeological Journal LV* 55 (1983): 61–67.

Golombek, Lisa. "The Draped Universe of Islam." In *Content and Context of Visual Arts in the Islamic World: Papers from a Colloquium in Memory of*

Richard Ettinghausen, edited by Priscilla P. Soucek, 25–39. University Park, PA: Pennsylvania State University Press, 1988.

Gonosová, Anna. "The Formation and Sources of Early Byzantine Floral Semis and Floral Diaper Patterns Reexamined." *Dumbarton Oaks Papers* 41 (1987): 227–237.

Gordon, Stewart, ed. *Robes and Honor: The Medieval World of Investiture.* New York: Palgrave, 2001.

Grant, Lindy. "The Coronation Mantle and the Westminster Sanctuary Pavement." *Mediaeval Journal* 4, no. 1 (2014): 1–21.

Grant, Lindy and Richard Mortimer. *Westminster Abbey: The Cosmati Pavements.* Aldershot: Ashgate, 2002.

Greene, J. Patrick. *Medieval Monasteries.* London: Leicester University Press, 1992.

Harrison, David. *The Bridges of Medieval England: Transport and Society, 400–1800.* Oxford: Clarendon Press, 2007.

Harvey, Sally. *Domesday: Book of Judgement.* Oxford: Oxford University Press, 2014.

Henderson, George. "Romance and Politics on Some Medieval English Seals." *Art History* I, no. 1 (1978): 26–42.

Hildebrandt, Berit and Carole Gillis. *Silk: Trade and Exchange Along the Silk Roads Between Rome and China in Antiquity.* Oxford: Oxbow Books, 2017.

Hillenbrand, Robert. "What Happened to the Sasanian Hunt in Islamic Art?" In *The Rise of Islam*, edited by Vesta Sarkhosh Curtis and Sarah Stewart, 84–101. London: I. B. Tauris, 2009.

Hodgson, Natasha R. "Lions, Tigers, and Bears: Encounters with Wild Animals and Bestial Imagery in the Context of Crusading to the Latin East." *Viator* 44, no. 1 (2013): 65–93.

Hoffman, Eva. "Pathways of Portability: Islamic and Christian Interchange from the Tenth through the Twelfth Century." *Art History* 24, no. 1 (2001): 17–50.

"Between East and West: The Wall Paintings of Samarra and The Construction of Abbasid Princely Culture." *Muqarnas* 25 (2008): 107–132.

Howell, Margaret. *Eleanor of Provence: Queenship in Thirteenth-Century England.* Oxford: Malden, 1998.

Hu, Jun. "Global Medieval at the 'End of the Silk Road,' circa 756 CE: The Shōsō-in Collection in Japan." *The Medieval Globe* 3, no. 2 (2017): 177–202.

Jacoby, David. "Silk Crosses the Mediterranean." In *Byzantium, Latin Romania, and the Mediterranean*, 55–79. Aldershot: Variorum, 2001.

Silk Economics and Cross-cultural Artistic Interaction: Byzantium, the Muslim World, and the Christian West." *Dumbarton Oaks Papers* 58 (2004): 197–240.

James, Thomas Beaumont. *The Palaces of Medieval England, c.1050–1550: Royalty, Nobility, the Episcopate, and Their Residences from Edward the Confessor to Henry VIII.* London: Seaby, 1990.

Keen, Laurence. "The Chapter House Decorated Tile Pavement." In *Westminster Abbey Chapter House: The History, Art and Architecture of "a Chapter House beyond Compare,"* edited by Warwick Rodwell and Richard Mortimer, 209–236. London: Society of Antiquaries of London, 2010.

Kim, Dorothy. "White Supremacists Have Weaponized an Imaginary Viking Past. It's Time to Reclaim the Real History." *Time* (2019). https://time .com/5569399/viking-history-white-nationalists/.

Kim, Hongnam. "An Analysis of the Early Unified Silla Bas-relief of Pearl Roundel, Tree of Life, Peacocks, and Lion from the Gyeongju National Museum, Korea." *The Silk Road* 15 (2017): 116–133.

Klein, Holger. "Eastern Objects and Western Desires: Relics and Reliquaries Between Byzantium and the West." *Dumbarton Oaks Papers* 58 (2004): 283–314.

Knicely, Carol. "Food for Thought in the Souillac Pillar: Devouring Beasts, Pain and the Subversion of Heroic Codes of Violence." *RACAR: revue d'art canadienne / Canadian Art Review* 24, no. 2 (1997): 14–37.

Lancaster, R. Kent. "Artists, Suppliers and Clerks: The Human Factors in the Art Patronage of Henry III." *Journal of the Warburg and Courtauld Institutes* 35 (1972): 81–107.

Lapina, Elizabeth, April Jehan Morris, Susanna A. Throop, and Laura J. Whatley. "Introduction." In *The Crusades and Visual Culture*, edited by Elizabeth Lapina, April Jehan Morris, Susanna A. Throop and Laura J. Whatley, 1–14. Aldershot: Ashgate, 2015.

Lehmann-Brockhaus, Otto. *Lateinische Schriftquellen zur Kunst in England, Wales und Schottland, vom Jahre 901 bis zum Jahre 1307.* Vols. 5 Munich: Prestel, 1955.

Leson, Richard. "'Partout la figure du lion': Thomas of Marle and the Enduring Legacy of the Coucy Donjon Tympanum." *Speculum* 93, no. 1 (2018): 27–71.

Lester, Anne. "Intimacy and Abundance: Textile Relics, the Veronica, and Christian Devotion in the Aftermath of the Fourth Crusade." *Material Religion* 14, no. 4 (2018): 533–544.

Lethaby, William Richard. "The Romance Tiles of Chertsey Abbey." *Annual Volume of the Walpole Society* 2 (1913): 69–80.

Westminster Abbey Re-Examined. London: Duckworth, 1925.

Lewis, Suzanne. *The Art of Matthew Paris in the Chronica Majora*. Berkeley: University of California Press, 1987.

Lipton, Sara. *Images of Intolerance: The Representation of Jews and Judaism in the Bible moralisée*. Berkeley: University of California Press, 1999.

Loomis, Roger Sherman. "Richard Coeur de Lion and the Pas Saladin in Medieval Art." *PMLA* 30, no. 3 (1915): 509–528. www.mla.org/ Publications/Journals/PMLA.

Illustrations of Medieval Romance on Tiles from Chertsey Abbey. Urbana: University of Illinois, 1916.

Luard, Henry Richards, ed. *Matthaei Parisiensis, Monachi Sancti Albani, Chronica Majora*. London: Longman, 1872.

Luyster, Amanda. "Reassembling Textile Networks: Treasuries and Re-collecting Practices in Thirteenth-Century England." *Speculum* 96, no. 4 (2021): 1039–1078.

ed. *Bringing the Holy Land Home: The Crusades, Chertsey Abbey, and the Reconstruction of a Medieval Masterpiece*. London: Harvey Miller, 2022.

"Fragmented Tile, Fragmented Text: Richard the Lionheart on Crusade and the Lost Latin Texts of the Chertsey Combat Tiles (c.1250)." *Digital Philology* 11, no. 1 (2022): 86–120.

English Bodies, Imported Silks: The Impact of Islamic and Byzantine Textiles in Gothic England. Forthcoming.

Mackie, Louise W. *Symbols of Power: Luxury Textiles from Islamic Lands, 7th–21st Century*. Cleveland: Cleveland Museum of Art, 2015.

Mann, Vivian B. "Samson vs. Hercules: A Carved Cycle of the Twelfth Century." *ACTA* 7 (1980 [1983]): 1–38.

Meister, Michael W. "The Pearl Roundel in Chinese Textile Design." *Ars Orientalis* 8 (1970): 255–267.

Meuwese, Martine. "Antioch and the Crusaders in Western Art." In *East and West in the Medieval Eastern Mediterranean. 1 Antioch from the Byzantine Reconquest until the End of the Crusader Principality*, edited by K. Ciggaar and M. Metcalf, 337–355. Leuven: Peeters, 2006.

Mittman, Asa Simon. *Maps and Monsters in Medieval England*. New York: Routledge, 2008.

Morrison, Elizabeth. *Book of Beasts: The Bestiary in the Medieval World*. Los Angeles: The J. Paul Getty Museum, 2019.

Morrison, Elizabeth and Anne D. Hedeman. *Imagining the Past in France: History in Manuscript Painting, 1250–1500*. Los Angeles: J. Paul Getty Museum, 2010.

Muthesius, Anna. *Byzantine Silk Weaving: AD 400 to AD 1200*. Vienna: Fassbaender, 1997.

Mynors, R. A. B., Rodney M. Thomson, and Michael Winterbottom, eds. *Gesta regum Anglorum = The History of the English Kings*. Vol. 1, Oxford Medieval Texts. Oxford: Clarendon Press, 1998.

Neilson, George. *Trial by Combat: From before the Middle Ages to 1819 A.D.* Boston: G.A. Jackson, 1909.

Noppen, J. G. *The Chapter House, Westminster Abbey.* Department of the Environment guidebook, revised by S. E. Rigold, London: H.M.S.O, 1952. https://catalogue.nla.gov.au/catalog/3890331.

Norton, Christopher. "The Medieval Tile Pavements of Winchester Cathedral." In *Medieval Art & Architecture at Winchester Cathedral*, edited by Thomas A. Heslop and Veronica A. Sekules, 78–93. Leeds, 1983.

"The Medieval Tile Pavements of Winchester Cathedral." In *Winchester Cathedral : Nine Hundred Years, 1093–1993*, edited by John Crook, 167–176. Chichester: Phillimore, 1993.

"The Luxury Pavement in England before Westminster." In *Westminster Abbey – The Cosmati Pavements*, edited by Lindy Grant and R. Mortimer, 7–27, 73–91. Aldershot: Ashgate, 2002.

Owen-Crocker, Gale R. and Elizabeth Coatsworth. *Encyclopedia of Dress and Textiles in the British Isles, c. 450–1450*. Leiden: Brill, 2012.

Paul, Nicholas. *To Follow in Their Footsteps: The Crusades and Family Memory in the High Middle Ages*. Ithaca: Cornell University Press, 2012.

Perella, Nicolas James. *The Kiss Sacred and Profane, An Interpretative History of Kiss Symbolism and Related Religio-Erotic Themes*. Berkeley: University of California Press, 1969.

Poulton, Rob. *Archaeological Investigations on the Site of Chertsey Abbey.* Research Volume of the Surrey Archaeological Society. Vol. 11, Guildford: Surrey Archaeological Society, 1988.

Prestwich, John Oswald. "Richard Coeur de Lion: Rex Bellicosus." In *Richard Coeur de Lion in History and Myth*, edited by Janet L. Nelson, 1–16. London: Centre for Late Antique and Medieval Studies, King's College, 1992.

Prestwich, Michael. *Armies and Warfare in the Middle Ages: The English Experience*. New Haven: Yale University Press, 1996.

Reeve, Matthew M. "The Painted Chamber at Westminster, Edward I, and the Crusade." *Viator* 37 (2006): 189–221.

Robertson, Roland. "Glocalization: Time-Space and Homogeneity-Heterogeneity." In *Global Modernities*, edited by Roland Robertson, Scott Lash, and Mike Featherstone, 25–44: Sage, 1995.

"Glocalization." *The International Encyclopedia of Anthropology* (2018): 1–8.

Schrenk, Sabine. *Textilien des Mittelmeerraumes aus spatantiker bis fruhislamischer Zeit.* Riggisberg: Abegg-Stiftung, 2004.

Shalem, Avinoam. *The Chasuble of Thomas Becket.* Munich: Hirmer Verlag, 2016.

Shaw, Henry. *Specimens of Tile Pavements Drawn from Existing Authorities.* London: B. M. Pickering, 1858.

Smith, John Masson. "Ayn Jālūt: Mamlūk Success or Mongol Failure?" *Harvard Journal of Asiatic Studies* 44, no. 2 (1984): 307–345.

Smith, Mary Frances, Robin Fleming, and Patricia Halpin. "Court and Piety in Late Anglo-Saxon England." *Catholic Historical Review* 87, no. 4 (2001): 569–602.

Strickland, Debra Higgs. *Saracens, Demons, and Jews: Making Monsters in Medieval Art.* Princeton: Princeton University Press, 2003.

Stubbs, William, ed. *Itinerarium peregrinorum et gesta regis Ricardi*, Rolls Series. London: Longmans, 1864.

Surrey Record Society. *Chertsey Abbey Cartularies, Volume II, Part 1, Being the Second Portion of the Cartulary in the Public Record Office.* Vol. XII (continued), London: Butler & Tanner for the Surrey Record Society, 1958.

Sweetenham, Carol. *Robert the Monk's History of the First Crusade = Historia Iherosolimitana.* Abingdon: Routledge, 2016.

"'Hoc enim non fuit humanum opus, sed divinum': Robert the Monk's Use of the Bible in the Historia Iherosolimitana." In *The Uses of the Bible in Crusader Sources*, edited by Elizabeth Lapina and Nicholas Morton, 133–151. Leiden: Brill, 2017.

Sweetenham, Carol and Linda M. Paterson. *The Canso d'Antioca: An Occitan Epic Chronicle of the First Crusade.* Burlington: Ashgate, 2003.

Taragan, Hana. "Textiles in Cross-cultural Encounters: The Case of the Umayyad Palace at Khirbat al-Mafjar." *Al-Masāq*, 32, no. 2 (2020): 140–155.

Thomas, Phillip Drennon. "The Tower of London's Royal Menagerie." *History Today* 46, no. 8 (1996): 29–35.

Tolley, Thomas. "Eleanor of Castile and the 'Spanish' Style in England." In *England in the Thirteenth Century: Proceedings of the 1989 Harlaxton Symposium*, 167–192: Stamford Watkins, 1991.

Toms, Elsie, ed. *Chertsey Abbey Court Rolls Abstract; Being a Calendar of Lansdowne Ms. Number 434 in the British Museum.* Vol. XXXVIII, Surrey Record Society. Frome: Printed by Butler & Tanner for the Surrey Record Society, 1937.

Trilling, James. *The Medallion Style: A Study in the Origins of Byzantine Taste.* New York: Garland, 1985.

"Medieval Interlace Ornament: The Making of a Cross-cultural Idiom." *Arte Medievale* 9, no. 1 (1995): 51–86.

Ornament: A Modern Perspective. Seattle: University of Washington Press, 2003.

Tristram, Ernest William. *English Medieval Wall Painting*. London: Oxford University Press, 1944.

Vida, Tivadar. *Late Antique Metal Vessels in the Carpathian Basin: Luxury and Power in the Early Middle Ages*. Budapest: Archaeolingua Alapítvány, 2016.

Vorderstrasse, Tasha. "Trade and Textiles from Medieval Antioch." *Al-Masaq-Islam and the Medieval Mediterranean* 22, no. 2 (2010): 151–171.

Walker, Alicia. *The Emperor and the World: Exotic Elements and the Imaging of Middle Byzantine Imperial Power, Ninth to Thirteenth Centuries C.E.* Cambridge: Cambridge University Press, 2012.

Watt, James C. Y., Anne E. Wardwell, and Morris Rossabi. *When Silk Was Gold: Central Asian and Chinese Textiles*. New York: Metropolitan Museum of Art in cooperation with the Cleveland Museum of Art, 1997.

Weiss, Daniel. "Biblical History and Medieval Historiography: Rationalizing Strategies in Crusader Art." *MLN* 108, no. 4 (1993): 710–737. www.press.jhu.edu/journals/mln.

Whatley, Laura. "Romance, Crusade, and the Orient in King Henry III of England's Royal Chambers." *Viator* 44, no. 3 (2013): 175–198.

White, Cynthia. *From the Ark to the Pulpit: An Edition and Translation of the "Transitional" Northumberland Bestiary (13th Century)*. Louvain-la-Neuve: Université Catholique de Louvain, 2009.

Wight, Jane A. *Mediaeval Floor Tiles: Their Design and Distribution in Britain*. London: J. Baker, 1975.

Williams, Elizabeth Dospěl. "A Taste for Textiles: Designing Umayyad and 'Abbāsid Interiors.'" In *Catalogue of the Textiles in the Dumbarton Oaks Byzantine Collection*, edited by Gudrun Bühl and Elizabeth Dospěl Williams. Washington, DC: www.doaks.org/resources/textiles/essays/williams, 2019.

Williamson, Paul. "Capitals from Chertsey Abbey." *Burlington Magazine* Feb 130, (1988): 124–127.

Wilson, Christopher. "A Monument to St Edward the Confessor: Henry Ill's Great Chamber at Westminster and Its Paintings." In *Westminster: II. The Art, Architecture and Archaeology of the Royal Palace*, edited by Warwick Rodwell and Tim Tatton-Brown. British Archaeological Association Conference Transactions, 2015.

Wyon, Alfred Benjamin and Allan Wyon. *The Great Seals of England, from the Earliest Period to the Present Time, Arranged and Illustrated with Descriptive and Historical Notes*. London: E. Stock, 1887.

Cambridge Elements ☰

The Global Middle Ages

Geraldine Heng

University of Texas at Austin

Geraldine Heng is Perceval Professor of English and Comparative Literature at the University of Texas, Austin. She is the author of *The Invention of Race in the European Middle Ages* (2018) and *England and the Jews: How Religion and Violence Created the First Racial State in the West* (2018), both published by Cambridge University Press, as well as *Empire of Magic: Medieval Romance and the Politics of Cultural Fantasy* (2003, Columbia). She is the editor of *Teaching the Global Middle Ages* (2022, MLA), coedits the University of Pennsylvania Press series, RaceB4Race: Critical Studies of the Premodern, and is working on a new book, Early Globalisms: The Interconnected World, 500–1500 CE. Originally from Singapore, Heng is a Fellow of the Medieval Academy of America, a member of the Medievalists of Color, and Founder and Co-director, with Susan Noakes, of the Global Middle Ages Project: www.globalmiddleages.org.

Susan J. Noakes

University of Minnesota – Twin Cities

Susan J. Noakes is Professor of French and Italian at the University of Minnesota – Twin Cities, where she also serves as Chair of the Department of French and Italian. For her many publications in French, Italian, and Comparative Literature, the University In 2009 named her Inaugural Chair in Arts, Design, and Humanities. Her most recent publication is an analysis of Salim Bachi's *L'Exil d'Ovide*, exploring a contemporary writer's reflection on his exile to Europe by comparing it to Ovid's exile to the Black Sea; it appears in *Salim Bachi*, edited by Agnes Schaffhauser, published in Paris by Harmattan in 2020.

About the Series

Elements in the Global Middle Ages is a series of concise studies that introduce researchers and instructors to an uncentered, interconnected world, c. 500–1500 CE. Individual Elements focus on the globe's geographic zones, its natural and built environments, its cultures, societies, arts, technologies, peoples, ecosystems, and lifeworlds.

Cambridge Elements ≡

The Global Middle Ages

Printed in the United States
by Baker & Taylor Publisher Services